PRAISE FOR *JE_____ _____*

"With deceptive ease Dr. Da_____ _____ o the Road to Emmaus for a few h_____ _____ d the Old Testament. With an envi_____ _____ s how to read the Old Testament as Christians. _____ book on Christ-centered biblical interpretation that doesn't involve complex grammatical, rhetorical, or hermeneutical complexities that cause the ordinary Christian (and pastor for that matter) to glaze over and despair. Rather, as a most agreeable companion, Professor Murray walks alongside us and points out the most important landmarks we need to notice if we are to make our way through the Old Testament for ourselves and see how it points to Christ. Far from talking down to us from the lofty heights of technical Old Testament scholarship (although he is familiar with them), he tells us that he once sat where most of us sit. But then, as a quality teacher, he is able to help us learn what he himself has so obviously done. Here, then, is an ideal primer for beginners, a great refresher course for anyone who has got lost in the woods attempting to read Scripture the Emmaus Road way, and a wonderful reminder to us all that it was Jesus himself who taught us that he is at the heart of the entire Bible, and not just the righthand side of it!"

—SINCLAIR B. FERGUSON, REDEEMER THEOLOGICAL
SEMINARY, DALLAS, TEXAS.

"This is not a small book, it is a game-changer. I read it with a notepad in one hand and at times tears on every page. If you think that we have to wait until that night in Bethlehem to meet Jesus face-to-face, this profound work shows that from the first chapter of Genesis to the final notes of John's Revelation, Jesus is on every page of God's love story. This is a book I will read over and over. I highly recommend it!"

—SHEILA WALSH, SINGER, BEST-SELLING AUTHOR,
SPEAKER WITH WOMEN OF FAITH CONFERENCES

"Certainly one of the most helpful and most needed new books that I have seen for a long while. True faith in Christ as revealed in the Old Testament needs to be grounded on right principles of interpretation. Whenever those principles are confused, faith in large portions of Scripture will also be confused. This book is more than a devotional read. It leads us to understand more accurately why Jesus could say of the scriptures, 'they testify of me'. What could be more important?"

—IAIN H. MURRAY, PASTOR, AUTHOR, AND EDITORIAL
DIRECTOR OF THE BANNER OF TRUTH PUBLISHERS

"Far too much Old Testament preaching is moralism—pure and simple. Moralism is an evil, wicked thing that suggests that with a little effort, and some help from the Spirit, we can improve our lot. Thus hundreds of 'killer-be' sermons ('Be like x or y') have urged Christians to ethical response without gospel foundations, encouraging guilt eradication by more urgent effort on our part. Failing to see the grand, 'eye in the sky' redemptive story of Scripture, such myopic views focus instead on self—self-effort, self-importance, self-justification. And Christians are rightly crying 'foul' to this pernicious trajectory, consigning to the dustbin of error where it belongs and replacing it with a Christ-centered, gospel-focused understanding of the Old Testament. There have been strident voices urging us to see Christ in the Old Testament in recent years—among them Greidanus, Goldsworthy, Clowney, and Chapell. Now comes David Murray's *Jesus on Every Page*—a bang-on target, concise summary of this urgently needed, hermeneutical adjustment. I cannot recommend it highly enough."

—Derek W. H. Thomas, Professor of Systematic Theology, RTS Atlanta; Minister of Preaching and Teaching, First Presbyterian Church, Columbia, South Carolina

"There's no one I'd rather have serve as my guide for a journey down the Emmaus road than David Murray. *Jesus on Every Page* provides solid, understandable categories and tools for retraining ourselves on how to read and understand the Old Testament. Without complicated theological jargon, this book helps readers to see that Jesus, in his person and work, is the answer to all of the Old Testament's lingering questions, the fulfillment of all of its unfulfilled promises, and the resolution to all of its unresolved tensions."

—Nancy Guthrie, author of the *Seeing Jesus in the Old Testament* Bible study series

"There could scarcely be a more worthy pursuit than seeking to learn of Jesus in the pages of Scripture. And—even allowing for the many differences in approach and interpretation—it would be difficult indeed to find a more accessible, concise, practically helpful, warm-hearted guide than David Murray's *Jesus On Every Page*."

—Fred G. Zaspel, Reformed Baptist Church, Franconia, Pennsylvania; Calvary Baptist Seminary, Lansdale, Pennsylvania

"In this book, seminary professor David Murray takes us on a fascinating journey to find the right kind of help in interpreting the Old Testament Christologically. Without sending us down any dubious interpretative avenues, David shows us not only that Jesus is on every page of the Old Testament, but in every picture, poem, historical fact, and prophetic utterance. His aim throughout is to remind New Testament Christians that they are whole Bible believers, and to give them a key to reading the Old Testament biblically. The key to his own book is simple enough: it is that the gospel interprets the Old Testament. As he unpacks this theme, David shows us that Jesus does not simply emerge at the end of the historical process we call the Old Testament, but was present from the outset as the Savior of sinners. This is a safe guide to a controversial topic, and will be of help both to theology students and serious Bible readers. I wish it a wide circulation, if only because it will enable a new generation of believers, many of whom don't really know how to handle the first half of the Bible, to read and preach the Old Testament just as its Author intended."

—Dr. Iain D. Campbell, author, adjunct professor at Westminster Seminary, and pastor of Point Free Church of Scotland

"Much has been written for seminary students and pastors on interpreting all of Scripture with a view to Christ. Unfortunately, very little has been written with the average Christian in mind. In *Jesus on Every Page*, David Murray sets out to correct this deficiency by sharing his own journey of discovery and providing ten simple ways to see Christ in the Old Testament. No longer is the person in the pew left to wonder how the preacher got to Jesus from that text in Leviticus about dietary restrictions; she will be able to make the connections herself. I hope you will read *Jesus on Every Page* and embark on your own 'Emmaus road' and discover that the entire Bible, both Old and New Testaments, tells the story of Jesus."

—Juan Sanchez, preaching pastor, Highpointe Baptist Church, Austin, Texas

"Every wise mountaineer, unless he is an expert, welcomes whatever help he can get to further his endeavor to reach the summit. Similarly, the Christian, as he daily studies his Bible, strives in his reading to get to know Christ more perfectly. Though he realizes that the summit of perfection will only be reached in heaven at last, he welcomes the helping hand of those ahead of him. Dr. David Murray has here given us all a welcome lift so that we might see Jesus much more clearly in the Old Testament. It cannot but be a sweet and an enlightening experience to be taught to know Jesus more perfectly."

—Maurice Roberts, author, pastor in the Free Church of Scotland

"With contagious delight, David Murray not only opens up the Old Testament beautifully, he draws you to marvel at the One it is all about. This is a moving, rich book that can hardly fail to help readers enjoy Jesus more in his Word."

—Michael Reeves, head of theology, Universities and Colleges Christian Fellowship; author of *Delighting in the Trinity*

"Jesus is indeed on every page, and Murray's book offers a practical, accessible, and engaging introduction to the Old Testament. The book not only helps Bible students to understand the excitement of the Old Testament's testimony to Christ, but provides a host of suggestions and paths by which readers can begin to experience for themselves the opening of depths in the Old Testament. This book shows the glory of Christ, and is recommended especially for anyone previously intimidated by the Old Testament."

—VERN S. POYTHRESS, PhD, ThD, PROFESSOR OF NEW TESTAMENT INTERPRETATION, WESTMINSTER THEOLOGICAL SEMINARY, PHILADELPHIA, PENNSYLVANIA

"If you heard that archeologists had discovered a genuine book with pictures of Jesus' life, a diary of his thoughts, and further explanation of his ministry, would you not yearn to have that book in your hands? If you have the Old Testament, you do! With the enthusiasm of personal discovery and the heart of a loving pastor, David Murray explains carefully and plainly that Jesus indeed can be seen, heard, and experienced on every page of the Old Testament."

—BARRY YORK, PASTOR AND PROFESSOR OF PRACTICAL THEOLOGY, REFORMED PRESBYTERIAN THEOLOGICAL SEMINARY

"With a multitude of hermeneutical challenges facing the church in the twenty-first century, the establishment and defense of Christological principles of biblical interpretation is not least among those of foremost importance. Turning to the teaching of Christ and the Apostles, David Murray carefully explains the exegetical and biblical-theological rational for a Christological interpretation of the Old Testament. Murray takes the reader into the world of redemptive history to show how Christ is the epicenter of all Old Testament revelation—so that you, too, will see *Jesus on Every Page*."

—NICK BATZIG, NEW COVENANT PRESBYTERIAN CHURCH, RICHMOND HILL, GEORGIA

"David Murray's *Jesus on Every Page* is the missing piece in most approaches to hermeneutics. A piece so central and important that without it the picture Scripture paints is incomplete and marred. Dr. Murray guides the reader safely through the Old Testament pointing to the Son of God who is there in person and promise. I can't imagine a clearer or more helpful book that shows us what Jesus meant when he said the Law, the Prophets, and Psalms all speak of his person and work."

—JOE THORN, AUTHOR OF *NOTE TO SELF: THE DISCIPLINE OF PREACHING TO YOURSELF*; LEAD PASTOR, REDEEMER FELLOWSHIP, ST. CHARLES, ILLINOIS

JESUS

ON EVERY PAGE

10 SIMPLE WAYS *to* SEEK *and* FIND
CHRIST *in the* OLD TESTAMENT

DAVID MURRAY

THOMAS NELSON
Since 1798

NASHVILLE   DALLAS   MEXICO CITY   RIO DE JANEIRO

Published in Nashville, Tennessee, by Thomas Nelson. Thomas Nelson is a registered trademark of Thomas Nelson, Inc.

Thomas Nelson, Inc., titles may be purchased in bulk for educational, business, fund-raising, or sales promotional use. For information, please e-mail SpecialMarkets@ ThomasNelson.com.

Library of Congress Cataloging-in-Publication Data

Murray, David, 1966 May 28–
  Jesus on every page : 10 simple ways to seek and find Christ in the Old Testament / David Murray.
      p. cm.
  Includes bibliographical references and index.
  ISBN 978-1-4002-0534-9
1. Typology (Theology) 2. Bible. N.T.—Relation to the Old Testament. I. Title.
BT225.M87 2013
221.6'4—dc23   2012048748

Printed in the United States of America

HB 10.04.2023

Dedicated to (Rev.) Angus and Joan Smith. Thank you for giving me my lovely wife and for inspiring my love of Christ in the Old Testament.

Why look at the shadow when you possess the substance? . . . What artist studies a landscape in the grey dawn, when he may see it in the blaze of day? True. Yet such study has its advantages. It not seldom happens that a portrait brings to view certain shades of expression which we had not previously observed in the face of the veritable man; and when some magnificent form of architecture, or the serried ridges and rocky peaks of a mountain, have stood up between us and the lingering lights of day, though the minor beauties of fluted columns or frowning crags were lost in the shades of evening, yet, drawn in sharp clear outline against a twilight sky, the effect of the whole was more impressive than when eyed in the glare of noon. Thus it may be well, at least occasionally, to examine the Gospel in the broad shadows and strongly defined outlines of an old economy.

—THOMAS GUTHRIE, *The Gospel in Ezekiel*

CONTENTS

PREFACE

Jesus Christ is the towering figure of world history. As such, He casts a bright shadow not only forward over all post-Bethlehem history but also backward over all Old Testament history that led up to Him. He is the person to whom and from whom all history flows. His luminous shadow brightens both BC and AD, but it is especially the BC years we wish to explore in this book.

Jesus on Every Page is an accessible guide to the increasingly popular subject of Jesus in the Old Testament. Although much has been written to help pastors with preaching Jesus from the Old Testament, there is little that provides sound principles and practical help for the average Christian who wants to explore this important way of knowing Jesus through His Word.

As well as writing something accessible and useful to the wider church, I wanted to provide a resource that would cover a number of methods of knowing Jesus in the Old Testament. As you will see from the endnotes, many excellent books deal with one or two ways of interpreting the Old Testament with Jesus in view. Some are strong on typology, others emphasize narrative, while still others focus on the prophets or the Old Testament appearances of Christ. In *Jesus on Every Page* I've tried to gather in one place ten different ways of discovering and enjoying Jesus in the Old Testament.

Another thing I noticed was that many books did not help the reader start to do his or her own Christ-centered interpretation. There was a focus on either the theory or the end product, for example, a sermon. But the practical steps that would help a reader get from a text or chapter to Jesus were often missing. I've therefore tried to provide templates and step-by-step guides at various points to help the reader start practicing this wonderful way of enjoying Jesus in His Word.

In the first part of the book, I tell the story of my own Emmaus road—how the Lord gradually taught me to see more and more of Jesus in the Old Testament. I wanted to share not only the result of what the Lord has taught me but also how He patiently led me there. Jesus found me as He found His disciples: "foolish . . . and slow of heart to believe in all that the prophets have spoken."[1] However, He graciously expounded to me in all the Scriptures the things concerning Himself, until eventually my heart burned within me as He opened the Scriptures to me.

I continue to thread my story through the rest of the book, but part 2 focuses more on ten simple methods to use in seeking and finding Jesus in the Old Testament. I hope that by combining my testimony to Jesus' work in my own life with my understanding of His Word, you will also experience a strangely enjoyable spiritual heartburn as together we discover and enjoy *Jesus on Every Page*.[2]

PART 1

MY ROAD TO EMMAUS

CHAPTER 1

WHERE DID THE OLD TESTAMENT GO?

Y ou'll find our text this morning in the Old Testament . . ."
I know this is a rare announcement today, but when you
heard it last, what did you think?

Oh no! Not another historical lecture.

We're going to get a whipping with the law today.

Why? I came to church to hear about Jesus.

What do Israel and Babylon have to do with my family struggles?

Or maybe you didn't just think it. You said it or e-mailed
it to the pastor afterward. And pastors are feeling the pressure.
Some surveys put the ratio of Old Testament to New Testament
sermons at 1 to 10. Some would like it nearer 0 to 10.

But might this imbalance in the spiritual diet of most Christians explain many of the spiritual problems in the modern
church and in modern Christians? Or as theologian Gleason
Archer put it: "How can Christian pastors hope to feed their flock

on a well-balanced spiritual diet if they completely neglect the 39 books of Holy Scripture on which Jesus and all the New Testament authors received their own spiritual nourishment?"[1]

CHANGE OF DIET

It wasn't always like this. The church used to have a much more balanced diet. So how did we get here? Consider these reasons:

Liberalism. The sustained attack on the Old Testament by liberal scholars has shaken many Christians' confidence in this part of the Bible.

Ignorance. It is almost impossible to understand large parts of the Old Testament without knowledge of the historical context and geographical setting. This knowledge was once widespread, but many Christians now know little or nothing of biblical history.

Irrelevance. Some look at the historical and geographical details of the Old Testament and wonder, what possible relevance can events and places from thousands of years ago have for me? And anyway, the New Testament teaches that many Old Testament practices have stopped. So, why study them?

Dispensationalism. Although unintended, the dispensational division of Scripture into different eras tends to relegate the Old Testament to a minor role in the life of the church and of the individual Christian.

Bad examples. Bad examples of Old Testament preaching and teaching are easy to find and even easier to ridicule. The malpractice of some, however, should not lead to the nonpractice of others.

Laziness. Studying the Old Testament is often more intellectually demanding than studying the New Testament. The familiar paths of the Gospels seem much more inviting than Leviticus, 2 Chronicles, or Nahum.

Christ-less preaching. Perhaps the greatest reason for so little interest in the Old Testament is that there has been so much Christ-less teaching from the Old Testament. At a popular level, Old Testament preaching has often degenerated into mere moralism, for example, "ten lessons from the life of Moses." At an academic level, there seems to be a determination to downplay and even remove any possibility of Christ-centeredness in the Old Testament. Little surprise that many turn away from the Old Testament and toward the New in order to find and enjoy Jesus.

Official, not personal. Although in recent years some preachers and teachers have worked harder at showing the Son of God's presence and work in the Old Testament, their efforts have often failed to satisfy because of the technically correct decision to use the official title *Christ* rather than the personal name *Jesus* in their Old Testament sermons and writings.

Jesus means "God saves," and it is the personal name given to the Son of God when He was born in Bethlehem two thousand years ago.

Christ means "anointed" or "sent and equipped by God," and it is the English translation of the Hebrew word *Messiah*. It's less personal—more of an official title or role like *president*—and is usually used when speaking of the Son of God prior to His earthly life.

One of my passions is to help Christians know Jesus more personally and intimately, so I decided to use *Jesus* as much as possible in this book. It not only brings Him closer to us than the official title; it reminds us that the Christ of the Old Testament is the same person as the Jesus of the New Testament.

When I use *Jesus* to speak of the Son of God's work in the Old Testament, I'm not saying that the man who was later born as Jesus was doing the work. I'm saying that the same person who was born as Jesus two thousand years ago was also at work in the Old Testament before then.

How Do We Get the Old Testament Back?

These are powerful and discouraging trends. How can we fight and even reverse them? We must combat liberal theology by treating the Old Testament as the inspired Word of God. We must patiently study biblical history and geography and learn how to profitably connect the past to the present. We must avoid the weaknesses of dispensationalism. We must identify and avoid bad practices, as well as search for, value, and learn from good preaching and teaching models. And we must be willing to put in the hours, the sweat, the toil, and the tears as we break up the long-untilled ground of the Old Testament. Above all, despite the prevalence of Christ-less moralism and the pressures of Christ-less academia, we must strive to find and enjoy Jesus in the Old Testament. That alone makes Old Testament study profitable and enjoyable. We can also minimize the disconnect caused by the overuse of *Christ* and bring Jesus nearer by using His personal name more than His official title.

It looks like a long and hard way back. Is it worth the effort? I believe it is. A few years ago I started to walk this difficult path; I learned a lot of valuable lessons along the way, and I'd like to share them with you. Let me begin by telling you about my own road to Emmaus.

CHAPTER 2

WHAT'S THE OLD TESTAMENT ALL ABOUT?

I spent the first ten years of my life in the Baptist church, where both of my parents were converted to Jesus. In my early teens, my father moved our family to the Presbyterian church. But a question puzzled me in both churches: *What's the Old Testament all about?* As far as I can remember, apart from Bible stories in Sunday school, we rarely opened the Old Testament in the Baptist church. And although we did open it from time to time in the Presbyterian church, I would probably have been less confused if we had left it shut.

I couldn't figure it out. We heard Old Testament stories in Sunday school but hardly ever in sermons. Or if we did, it seemed more like a history lesson about distant, dusty places and people rather than anything relevant and useful for my life. What was the Old Testament all about? I knew the New Testament was about Jesus, but the Old Testament? Israel? The Law? Lots of blood and guts—animal and human?

Embarrassment and Apologies

Sometimes a preacher would make a fairly miraculous connection between the Old Testament and Jesus, but that seemed more like intellectual gymnastics or some spooky numbers gig. Admittedly I was not converted and had little interest in the gospel, but my fundamental impression was that the Old Testament was a bit of an embarrassment to everyone and that usually we referred to it only to apologize for it or contrast it with the New Testament.

When the Lord graciously saved me in my early twenties, I started reading the Bible as I'd never done before. But even then, most of my reading was in the New Testament. Any Old Testament study was centered on my interest in the creation-versus-evolution debate in Genesis 1–2.

When I was converted, my mother shared her group Bible study on Joshua with me, just to help me start reading my Bible. It was interesting but not very enlightening. Was I to get an army together and start driving out the heathen in Glasgow? Joshua did have the Hebrew name for Jesus, but that didn't get me very far either.

Eventually I got into the Gospels, and Jesus soon became very real and precious to me. My study really just confirmed to me the seeming uselessness of the Old Testament.

Niggle, Niggle

And yet something still niggled away at me. Why would God have given us the majority of the Bible in the Old Testament?

I was repeatedly drawn to the book of Proverbs and kept reading there about "the fear of the Lord" being the beginning of wisdom. I was on a mission trip in Hungary at the time, and I asked the group I was traveling with if we should fear the Lord. The whole minibus jumped down my throat. "Of course not. That's Old Testament religion!" they exclaimed.

I sheepishly closed those dated and irrelevant Proverbs and returned to the safe ground of John's gospel. And that's where I stayed for a few years, with a few Epistles thrown in as well.

But the niggle still niggled, especially when I started listening to my future father-in-law, Angus Smith, preaching powerful Christ-centered sermons from the Old Testament. I couldn't quite figure out the *why* or the *how*, but it seemed much more plausible and reasonable than anything I'd heard before. In fact, it sounded like the same gospel as the New Testament.

Golden Keys?

When I felt called to the ministry, I entered a Presbyterian seminary and looked forward to finding the golden keys to Old Testament interpretation. I was sorely disappointed: lots of Hebrew and lots of technical work with the text but not one key. The Old Testament still seemed to represent a very different religion from the Christ-centered one I'd come to love through reading the New Testament. After a particularly tedious lecture on the sacrificial ritual, I did venture to ask how to preach a "Christian sermon" from such texts only to be told, "That's for you to figure out."

I was still trying to preach Old Testament sermons from time to time, but they were more of the gymnastic, "spooky numbers" variety than my father-in-law's approach. Mostly I avoided them, not wanting to pass on my confusion to others.

Then my denomination asked me to become our professor of Hebrew and Old Testament.

THE SHORT STRAW

Yes, you read that right. I was in a small Scottish Presbyterian denomination, and we wanted to start our own seminary to train our students for the ministry. But our church couldn't find anyone to teach Hebrew and Old Testament, especially the Hebrew part. Because I was one of the most recent graduates from seminary and therefore could at least recognize the Hebrew alphabet, I was pressured into accepting this part-time post. I still remember a godly elderly pastor cornering me and saying, "David, if you don't do it, we can't have a seminary."

I returned home from these church meetings with a mixture of disbelief, anger, fear, and confusion. I'd just been appointed to teach our students Hebrew and Old Testament, and yet I hardly knew anything about either. I remember saying to some of the other newly appointed lecturers, "Well, I got the short straw, didn't I?" They nodded . . . and laughed.

Looking back, I now see that though it was a highly unconventional path to training pastors, it was the Lord's way of forcing me into studying the Old Testament as I had never done before and never would have without this motivation.

FIRST STEPS ON THE EMMAUS ROAD

I started contacting seminaries throughout the world to ask them for any Old Testament courses they could send me. Multiple large boxes of books started arriving from Amazon as I clicked "Buy" on anything that looked remotely helpful. Eighteen-hour days became the norm for years as I tried to balance a busy pastorate with this new "burden."

Lo and behold, the subject I dreaded, I started to enjoy. Yes, many of the books and courses were similar to some of the confused teaching I'd already been exposed to, but here and there I discovered some long-sought-after keys that began opening up the Old Testament and persuasively showing me Jesus in a way I'd never seen Him before.

I found the first gospel key on the Emmaus road.

CHAPTER 3

JESUS' ANSWER

For years, I'd been asking myself and anyone who would listen, "What's the Old Testament all about?" The Author, the divine Author behind the human authors, had already given the answer to similarly confused disciples about two thousand years ago. Jesus told them the Old Testament was all about *Him*.

Having patiently listened to His still-mourning disciples tell of their disappointed messianic hopes, the freshly resurrected Jesus intervened with a rebuke of their foolish ignorance and unbelief: "O foolish ones, and slow of heart to believe in all that the prophets have spoken! Ought not the Christ to have suffered these things and to enter into His glory?"[1]

Jesus told them that their account of His life and death matched exactly the predictions of the Old Testament prophets. They had believed *some* of the prophets' writings—the parts that spoke of the Messiah's glory. But they had not believed *all* that the prophets had spoken—especially the parts that spoke of the Messiah's sufferings and death.

Having rebuked their foolish ignorance, Jesus then gave the disciples a full interpretation of the Old Testament Scriptures *in the light of recent events.* That insight was a critical turning point for me. I had heard academics say again and again: "We must not use the New Testament to interpret the Old Testament." I know of one Old Testament professor who banned the use of the New Testament in his classroom. Talk about trying to study in the dark.

THE GOSPEL INTERPRETS THE OLD TESTAMENT

And yet here, Jesus Himself used New Testament light to interpret the Old Testament scriptures. He used the light of New Testament events to preach from the Old Testament. Old Testament scholar Graeme Goldsworthy wrote: "We do not start at Genesis 1 and work our way forward until we discover where it is all leading. Rather we first come to Christ, and he directs us to study the Old Testament in the light of the gospel. The gospel will interpret the Old Testament by showing us its goal and meaning."[2]

Jesus titled His Emmaus road sermon "The Things Concerning Himself." He took a big text—Moses, *all* the Prophets, and *all* the Scriptures. And it had two main points—His sufferings and His glory.[3] In other words, the whole Old Testament was about Him, specifically His sufferings and His glory.

I went back and started reading the Gospels again and discovered that this note didn't just emerge at the end of Jesus' ministry. Right from the start He presented Himself not as a complete contrast to the Old Testament but as its climax and fulfillment.[4] My daily Bible reading was filled with new excitement as I began to search the Scriptures to see if these things were so or if I'd taken another wrong turn. Soon, another gospel key landed in my lap.

ABRAHAM'S GOSPEL

"Abraham rejoiced to see My day, and he saw it and was glad."[5]

I'd read it many times before, but this time these words of Jesus transformed Abraham from a theistic Jew into a Christian brother. Abraham had more than a general belief in God; he had a joyful, Messiah-centered faith. I wanted to know more. When did Abraham see Jesus' day with joy?

Although Jesus did not answer that question in John 8, He gave us more details years later through the apostle Paul. Reflecting on God's promise to Abraham in Genesis 12, when He called him to leave Ur, Paul wrote, "The Scripture, foreseeing that God would justify the Gentiles by faith, *preached the gospel to Abraham* beforehand, saying, 'In you all the nations shall be blessed.'"[6] That call and promise are often portrayed as coming out of the blue. But remember, they were building on the already-known promise of a Redeemer who would bless the world by defeating Satan.[7] Abraham was being told, "The world-blessing Redeemer will come from your family." That's why Paul could say that God "preached the gospel to Abraham."

Genesis 12:1–3 was not the whole gospel, but on top of Genesis 3:15, it was enough of the gospel to enable Abraham to obey God's call by faith and to see Christ's day by faith and be glad.[8] And when that happy day finally came, both Mary and Zacharias rejoiced in it as the fulfillment of the promises given to Abraham.[9]

Paul repeatedly presented Abraham as the prototype and example of saving faith, which is not exactly motivational if he and we believe different gospels. But we don't. We all believe the same gospel. The vocabulary was different, the clarity was different (Abraham believed in the shadows; we, in the sunlight), and the direction was different (Abraham looked forward to Jesus, whereas we look back), but the core, the essence, the focus was the same. His faith wrapped itself around the promised Satan-crushing, world-blessing, life-giving Seed of the woman, just as ours does. And the result is also the same—"he believed in the LORD, and He accounted it to him for righteousness."[10]

"ME! ME! ME!"

The more I pursued this line of Bible study, the more my heart also burned and leaped with joy as I discovered Jesus on every page. He wasn't just here and there—He was everywhere.

But then I began to worry. Was I overreading the Bible? Was I getting carried away? Lots of books seemed to tell me so and even some of the pastors I was beginning to share this discovery with. Maybe I should just go back to the safe ground of the New Testament. Then, the clincher . . . from Jesus Himself: "You search the Scriptures, for in them you think you have eternal life; and these are they which testify of Me. . . . For if you believed Moses, you would believe Me; for he wrote about Me."[11]

"The Old Testament scriptures testify of Me . . . Moses wrote about Me . . . Believing Moses' teaching is the same as believing Me."

What's the Old Testament all about? Jesus' emphatic answer is "Me! Me! Me!"

But what about asking those who knew Jesus best? What did the apostles think the Old Testament was all about? Did they get it or miss it?

CHAPTER 4

PETER'S ANSWER

I was never very enthusiastic about preaching consecutively through books of the Bible, probably because I'd rarely seen it done very well. Everyone else was doing it, however, so I thought I should probably try it. I chose 1 Peter for no other reason than I had more commentaries on it than on any other epistle. Also, it was quite short, allowing me to escape relatively quickly if the series began to sink the listeners or me.

Little did I know that the Lord was about to provide another gospel key to finding Jesus in the Old Testament. I had only preached a couple of sermons when I came to 1 Peter 1:10–12. I discovered there that Peter totally agreed with Jesus: the Old Testament was all about Him.

PROPHETIC PREDICTIONS

The prophets made predictions, wrote Peter. No big surprise there. The surprise was how and what they predicted. The "Spirit of

Christ," the Holy Spirit, was in the prophets,[1] making the coming Christ "the primary focus of the Holy Spirit's activity in the Old Testament prophets."[2]

We shouldn't be surprised then to read that, like the New Testament apostles, the Old Testament prophets were focused on "salvation" and "prophesied of the grace that would come." And not only did they preach salvation by grace, but they also preached the way this would be accomplished—by a suffering Messiah. Through the prophets, the Spirit of Christ "testified beforehand the sufferings of Christ and the glories that would follow."[3]

But I wanted to know, where are these prophecies? Professor Wayne Grudem's answer took me into another dimension:

> If we are to look for examples of this predicting activity, we may in fact look through the whole of the Old Testament, for the New Testament authors can sometimes speak of the whole of the Old Testament as the writings of "the prophets." . . . In this sense the predictions of the sufferings of the Messiah begin with the prediction of the "seed" of the woman who would be bruised in the heel by the serpent (Gn. 3:15), and continue through much of the Old Testament writings. . . . Yet all these verses are only a beginning, for they do not include the "acted-out prophecies" seen in the historical events of the Old Testament, where in the lives of people like Abraham, Isaac, Jacob, Joseph, Moses, Joshua, David, Solomon, Jonah, and often the nation of Israel generally, God brought to pass events which foreshadowed a pattern of life that would be later followed by "one greater than Solomon," one who was David's greater Son.[4]

Then I started hearing the voices again, scholarly voices, warning voices: *Well, yes, David, we can look back and see what the prophets were predicting, but they didn't have a clue what they were talking about.* What did Peter say to that?

PROPHETIC RESEARCH

Peter told us *the prophets studied their predictions.* Because it was not always immediately or entirely clear to the prophets what their predictions meant, they "inquired and searched carefully" into the salvation they prophesied.[5] Specifically, they searched "what, or what manner of time, the Spirit of Christ who was in them was indicating when He testified beforehand the sufferings of Christ and the glories that would follow."[6] Their diligent and careful research into their own and previous prophecies was not vague and aimless but Christ centered. New Testament commentator J. Ramsey Michaels wrote: "Even though the prophets' ministry was long before the fact, Peter depicts them as pointing not to an undefined messianic figure but specifically to Jesus Christ. 'Christ' is a name to Peter rather than a title, and he writes as if the prophets viewed matters in the same way."[7]

When I was studying these verses, I noticed that some Bible versions mistranslated verse 11, suggesting that the prophets did not know either the person or the time they were predicting. I couldn't make sense of that as the surrounding verses in Peter showed that they knew a lot about the person. The prophets' questions were more about the exact timing and the specific circumstances of the fulfillment. Old Testament scholar Walter

Kaiser demonstrated from these verses in Peter that the prophets knew these things:

1. Jesus would come.
2. Jesus would suffer.
3. Jesus would be glorified (in kingly splendor).
4. The order of events was that the suffering came first, and then the glorious period followed.
5. This message had been revealed to the prophets not only for their own day, but also for a future generation.[8]

It's all there, in these few verses, and yet I'd missed it for so many years. Although the prophets did not have comprehensive and complete knowledge of Jesus (who does?), they knew enough to answer the *who* question. Their major questions were about the *when* and the *how*.

PROPHETIC PATIENCE

Peter then said *the prophets knew their predictions would be even better understood by future generations*. It was revealed to them that "not to themselves, but to us they were ministering the things which now have been reported to you through those who have preached the gospel to you by the Holy Spirit sent from heaven."[9]

Though the prophets grew in understanding of the Savior they were looking for, Peter told us they knew their predictions would fully make sense to their readers only when they happened. Old Testament professor Sidney Greidanus put it like this:

The power and grace of Christ's redemption are present in the Old Testament long before he is born. At the same time, Old Testament believers look forward to the coming of Christ, when they will receive "far more light." In the meantime, God gave many promises of the coming Messiah and raised up types that prefigured him.[10]

I initially assumed this meant the Old Testament presented only the broad, general characteristics of Jesus' person and work while the New Testament filled in the details. As I read and reread the Old Testament, I saw that while the New Testament is more detailed in some respects, the Old Testament is actually more detailed in other areas. For example, nowhere in the New Testament are we given such insight into the emotions and feelings of the Lord Jesus during His sufferings as we are in the prophetic Psalms 22 and 69. Likewise, Isaiah 53 contains considerable detail.

Peter was not so much teaching a lack of detail but expressing a lack of full understanding. And that lack was not due to a lack of spirituality or holiness; many of the predicted events could not be understood until they happened. Even Christ's disciples had limited understanding of the person and work of Christ until after His resurrection.

Peter then tied the Old Testament prophets and the New Testament apostles together. The same "things" that were predicted, studied, and partly understood by the prophets are now "reported to you through those who have preached the gospel to you by the Holy Spirit sent from heaven."

The prophets ministered the same "things" that the apostles "now reported." The Old Testament "things" and the New

Testament "reports" were identical in substance. The major difference, apart from the clothes that dressed up the truths, was that since Pentecost, the New Testament "reports" were accompanied by a greater measure of the "Holy Spirit sent down from heaven," giving the preaching greater power and better enlightening the minds of the hearers.[11]

It wasn't just Jesus who said the Old Testament was all about Him. Peter, one of those who knew Him best, puts his "amen" to that as well.

Okay, I thought, *let's wrap this up by quickly looking at how His other best friends wrote about Jesus in the Old Testament, just to make sure Peter hadn't picked up the wrong end of the stick, as he often did.* It was then that I started running into serious problems and my theory started falling apart.

CHAPTER 5

PAUL'S ANSWER

D id anyone, apart from Jesus, know the Old Testament better than Paul, a self-described "Hebrew of the Hebrews"?[1]

No.

What did Paul think it was all about?

Although in a number of passages Paul agreed that the Old Testament was all about Jesus and salvation, I started finding passages where he seemed to say it was all about law and condemnation.

Oh dear! Who's right: Jesus and Peter—or Paul?

I began to think: *Maybe the church's Old Testament confusion is justified.* I mean, if the apostles can't agree with one another, what hope do we have? If Paul can't be consistent with himself, then little wonder that we ordinary Christians end up tying ourselves in knots.

Despondent, I gave up for a while. Galatians 3–4 and 2 Corinthians 3 were simply too intimidating. I couldn't ignore them, yet I couldn't easily reconcile them with all I thought I'd been discovering. Maybe I'd made a big mistake, maybe many big mistakes.

But the Bible cannot contradict itself, and an inspired apostle cannot contradict himself. With trepidation I eventually started to study these scary passages. I didn't want to find out that my Christ-centered study of the Old Testament was just a mirage, but neither could I confidently teach or preach Jesus from the Old Testament until I honestly faced the difficulties of these passages.

I opened my Bible at Galatians 3 and prayed for light.

GALATIANS 3–4

There's no question that in parts of Galatians 3–4, Paul seemed to view the Old Testament, especially Old Testament law, in a very negative light. As I read these chapters more closely, however, I began to see Paul making a distinction between the Old Testament as rightly understood and the Old Testament as warped and perverted by Judaizing legalists.

This, to me, was the gospel key to understanding the seeming contradictions. Paul was not negative about the Old Testament as designed by God but about the Old Testament as perverted by man. And if anyone knew this difference, it was Paul the apostle of grace, who had been Saul the persecutor of grace.

Here's the background to these chapters. Through the Christ-centered preaching of the apostle Paul, the Galatians had been delivered from the bondage of trying to get to heaven by obeying the Ten Commandments and following the ceremonial law. Paul preached a Jesus who had obeyed the moral law for sinners, a Jesus who had suffered the penalty of a law broken by sinners, and a Jesus who had abolished the rituals and ceremonies by fulfilling them. And many Galatians believed in this Jesus. The yoke of bondage was smashed. The prison doors were opened. The chains fell off. They entered a new world of freedom and liberty. Who would ever give that up?

Yoke, Handcuffs, Padlock, Chains

The Galatians did. They allowed false teachers from the Jewish synagogue to persuade them that faith in Jesus was not enough. They needed to be circumcised. They needed to follow the ceremonial rituals. Turning away from Jesus, they put their necks under the heavy yoke again; they put the handcuffs on and padlocked their legs in chains.

Paul protested: "Tell me, you who desire to be under the law, do you not hear the law?"[2] If I may paraphrase this, Paul was saying: "Tell me, you who are trying to be saved by doing the law of Moses, have you not read what Moses wrote elsewhere?"

He then pointed them to Genesis 15–17 to show that it was never God's intention that sinners be saved by their own best efforts. He did so by using Abraham's two sons to illustrate two ways of salvation: "For it is written that Abraham had two sons: the one by a bondwoman, the other by a freewoman."[3]

The mother of the first child was Hagar, the slave. Her son, Ishmael, was "born according to the flesh," the result of foolish human reasoning and sinful human effort. The mother of the second child was Sarah, Abraham's wife. Her child, Isaac, was the result of God's promise.[4]

Paul called these two births "an allegory," a symbol or a living parable for two ways of relating to God.[5]

- The birth of Ishmael is a vivid illustration of relating to God by using the best human reasoning plus the best human effort. Ishmael is human effort apart from the divine promise. Ishmael is a symbol of man's helping hand for a helpless God.
- The birth of Isaac is an illustration of relating to God by trusting in His promise alone. Isaac is a symbol of man's helplessness reaching out for divine help.

Paul then changed the imagery a bit. He moved from the bedroom to a dusty, distant, desert mountain. He said that the Ishmael way of relating to God is similar to the covenant from Mount Sinai (coincidentally called Agar by the Arabs).[6] On the face of it, Paul seemed to be saying that when God entered into covenant with Israel at Sinai, He was initiating a fleshly way, a Hagar way of relating to Him. The people of Israel were to bring their best human reasoning and their best human effort. If that's what Paul was teaching here, it's no wonder that he could describe the Sinai covenant as "bondage."[7]

But Paul was not looking back at the Sinai covenant and portraying it as a legalistic bondage. He was looking at the way most Jews of his day had misunderstood the originally gracious Sinai covenant and perverted it into a covenant of works, resulting in bondage.

Theological Bomb and Gospel Key

In case you missed it, I've just dropped a theological bomb. I just said that God intended grace and revealed grace in the covenant with Israel at Sinai. Actually, although it seems like a bomb, it's really another gospel key, arguably the most important key, to discovering and enjoying Jesus in the Old Testament.

Let me put this as clearly and boldly as possible: given the huge place and role of the Sinai covenant in the Old Testament, if it's a legal covenant, a covenant of "do this and live," then we must slam the door on any hope of finding and enjoying Jesus and His salvation in the Old Testament. And let's throw away the gospel keys we've been carrying from Jesus and Peter.

But if it is a covenant of grace, a covenant of "believe and be saved," then truly we have a key to seeing Jesus on every page of the Old Testament. The stakes are high; indeed they couldn't be higher.

Although I was swimming against the tide of all I had been brought up with and most modern Christian views of Moses and Sinai, I gradually came to be totally and absolutely convinced that the Sinai covenant is a revelation of Jesus and His gracious salvation. Here are the four arguments that persuaded me:

Four Persuasive Arguments

First, *the Sinai covenant painted pictures of grace.* The moral law of Exodus 20 was preceded by the grace of the Passover lamb, concluded by the covenant ratification sacrifices, and followed by the gracious provision and acceptance of the sacrificial lambs in the ceremonial law.[8] God book-ended the obedience He required with multiple-picture sermons of the coming suffering Savior.

Second, *the Sinai covenant is set in the context of grace.* Exodus 19:4–5 sets forth all God had done in delivering Israel from Egypt as the basis for the divine "therefore obey": "You have seen what I did to the Egyptians, and how I bore you on eagles' wings and brought you to Myself. Now therefore, if you will indeed obey My voice and keep My covenant, then you shall be a special treasure to Me above all people."

Redemption brought the Israelites into a relationship with God, which they were to respond to with grateful obedience. Rather than "obey and you will be brought into relationship with Me by a great redemption," it was, "As you've been redeemed and brought into a relationship with Me, here are some rules to help you show your gratitude and keep our relationship happy and healthy."

And as if that wasn't enough, God underlined it again in Exodus 20 when, just before giving the moral law, He said: "I am the LORD your God [relationship], who brought you out of the land of Egypt [redemption]," before saying, "You shall . . . you shall not."[9] Again, redemption and relationship come before rules to help express thankfulness. Anglican pastor and Old Testament scholar Christopher Wright put it like this:

> The law was given to people whom God had already re-deemed. . . . Grace comes before the law. There are eighteen chapters of salvation before we get to Sinai and the Ten Commandments. . . . I stress this because the idea that . . . in the OT salvation was by obeying the law, whereas in the NT it is by grace, is a terrible distortion of Scripture.[10]

Third, *the Sinai covenant points to our need of grace.* In Galatians 3, Paul argued strongly that the law was not intended to disannul or cancel the promise of grace.[11] He began by asserting that the gospel of Abraham was a gospel of salvation by grace through faith in Jesus.[12] But he then went on to prove that the gospel of Moses was also a gospel of salvation by grace through faith in Jesus: "And this I say, that the law, which was four hundred and thirty years later, cannot annul the covenant that was confirmed before by God in Christ, that it should make the promise of no effect."[13]

He argued this from ordinary human experience. He said that even human covenants cannot be canceled or changed.[14] The implication is obvious: whatever the Sinai covenant did, it did not cancel or change the saving promises of grace to Abraham. As Paul wrote, "Is the law then against the promises of God? Certainly not!"[15]

If the law does not cancel, change, or even oppose the Abrahamic promises of grace, what purpose does it have?

Apart from revealing grace through the *pictures* of grace and the *context* of grace, as I have already stated, it also points to our *need* of grace: "What purpose then does the law serve? It was added because of transgressions, till the Seed should come to whom the promise was made."[16]

A large part of the law's purpose, especially the moral law element, was to bring us to see our desperate need for the promise and to lead us, as a disciplinary teacher, to the Promised One, "that we might be justified by faith."[17] The law of circumcision served the same purpose for Abraham. And now that Jesus has come and faith has come, there is no longer the same need for the ceremonies or for circumcision.[18]

Fourth, *the Sinai covenant shows how we are to respond to grace.* The great statements about God's gracious redemption bringing Israel into a gracious relationship with Him[19] are followed by a great, divine "therefore obey."[20] Having redeemed them and brought them into a relationship with Him, God gave them clear rules to help them show their gratitude to Him and keep their relationship healthy.

What grace, that God should guide His people in this way! And as if that was not enough, He promised rewards for obeying in response to His grace.[21] Many read these motivation clauses found throughout the Old Testament and say, "See, it's all about works and reward." But that fails to recognize that redemption and relationship came before any rules or reward. Christopher Wright stated: "Obedience is the only right response to having been saved, and the way to enjoy the fruits of redemption, not to earn them."[22]

The Sinai covenant then, rightly understood, was a revelation of grace. Or to put it another way, the gospel of Abraham was the gospel of Moses. And both were the gospel of Jesus.

Jesus even portrayed the glorified Abraham in heaven pointing sinners to Moses and the prophets for the way of salvation.[23] And we are told four times in Hebrews 11 that Moses walked by faith.[24] We are specifically told that he had saving faith in Jesus.[25] Was saved-by-grace Moses really going to institute a legalistic system that would turn sinners away from divine grace through the coming Savior to salvation through following ceremonies and trying our best? Never!

When Paul attacked the Sinai covenant, he was not attacking it as it was designed by God, but as it had been twisted and abused by the Jews. That perversion was Jerusalem's main religion when Paul was writing, and it brought the people into bondage.[26] Paul told the Galatians—and us—what to do with every attempt to mix law with grace, human effort with divine promise. Cast it out. Expel it. Instead, embrace the freedom and joy of the heavenly Jerusalem's religion of faith in the promise of grace.[27]

No mirage then. Paul was on the same page as Jesus and Peter in taking a Christ-centered approach to the Old Testament. But one other chapter in Paul's writings still troubled me.

2 CORINTHIANS 3:6–18

In 2 Corinthians 3:6–18, Paul again discussed the relationship between the Old and New Testaments, and on the face of it, he again seemed to portray them as opposites. He described the Old Testament and its effects using the following phrases: "the letter kills," "the ministry of death, written and engraved on stones," and "the ministry of condemnation."[28] His description of the New Testament was quite a contrast: "the Spirit gives life," "the ministry of the Spirit," and "the ministry of righteousness."[29]

I asked myself two questions about this comparison:

- Was Paul describing all the Old Testament or one part of it?

Because Paul was referring to what was "written and engraved on stones," I decided that he was not referring to the whole Old Testament or even to the whole law of Moses but to the moral law, the Ten Commandments, which we are specifically told were "written and engraved on stones."

- Paul said that the Ten Commandments killed and condemned. Is that what God designed, or was it, as

33

with the Galatians, the result of misunderstanding and misuse?

As we've already seen, the Sinai covenant taken as a whole is a revelation of grace. Here Paul taught that when the Ten Commandments are ripped from their gracious context and taken in isolation, when obedience to them is attempted without faith in Jesus or the work of the Holy Spirit, they become a condemning and killing letter. As Augustine put it, "If the Spirit of grace is absent, the law is present only to accuse and kill us."[30]

But Paul was not just concerned to expose the Jewish perversion of the old Sinai covenant. He also wanted to show its temporary and inferior nature, even as rightly understood, when compared to the new covenant. The fact that the shining glory on Moses' face gradually faded should indicate that the old covenant at Sinai was not God's last word. Paul said that the temporary nature of this glory was a parable for the whole Mosaic system. It was temporary and transient, designed to fade away and eventually be replaced by a system that would be far superior due to its clarity and permanence.[31]

Although grace was gloriously displayed in the predictive pictures of the old covenant, many people became attached to the pictures themselves, the sacrifices and ceremonies, rather than to the One pictured and prophesied in them. They took the husks and ignored the kernel. This focus on the physical and the visible obscured Jesus from them.

In contrast, the new covenant used "great plainness of speech."[32] It was the same message of grace, but the veil was "taken away in Christ."[33] Thus, when Jesus fulfilled the ceremonies, the symbols, and the shadows, He removed the need for these interim, relatively obscure measures.

Charles Hodge, the late principal of Princeton, put it succinctly in his commentary on this passage:

> The Old Testament Scriptures are intelligible only when understood as predicting and prefiguring Christ. . . . The knowledge of Christ, as a matter of fact and as a matter of course, removes the veil from the Old Testament. . . . The main idea of the whole context is, that the recognition of Jesus Christ as Lord, or Jehovah, is the key to the Old Testament. It opens all its mysteries, or, to use the figure of the apostle, it removes the veil that hid from the Jews the true meaning of their own Scriptures. As soon as they turn to the Lord, i.e., as soon as they recognize Jesus Christ as their Jehovah, then everything becomes bright and clear.[34]

Paul, this Hebrew of the Hebrews, viewed Christianity not as giving up Judaism but as embracing true Judaism. He was not turning away from Old Testament religion but embracing it as rightly understood. Paul was both a Hebrew of the Hebrews and a Christian of the Christians at one and the same time.

We're back on the road to Emmaus, I believe.

CHAPTER 6

JOHN'S ANSWER

W hat's the Old Testament all about?
Christ, Peter, and Paul agreed that it's all about Christ and
His salvation.

But there remains one holdout verse. And it's a big one
because it was written by the apostle John, Christ's best-loved
earthly friend. Although John recorded verses that support a
Christ-centered view of the Old Testament—for example, John
5:39, 46; 8:56—this one seems to totally contradict it: "For the
law was given through Moses, but grace and truth came through
Jesus Christ."[1] There you have it. All my previous pages are just
fit for the trash: Moses was law; Jesus was grace. Can't get much
clearer than that, can you?

But wait. Before you add this volume to the other useless
books gathering dust on your shelves, let me give you an illustration that will lay the groundwork for understanding what this
verse teaches about the relationship between the Old and the New
Testaments.

GRACE UNDER NEW MANAGEMENT

Some years ago, Office Administration, an office supplies business, was prospering through selling high-quality paper, envelopes, and pens to various local companies. With the advent of the personal computer and e-mail, however, demand for these products began to diminish. Unfamiliar with this new technology, the management decided to stick with the paper, envelopes, pens, and so on that had served them well in past years. Sales continued to plummet. Eventually their warehouses were full, but their order books were empty.

At that point, the managing director's son, who had been trying for some time to change the company's product range, offered to buy out the older management. A deal was concluded, and the son took over. The warehouses were emptied of old stock, and in came personal computers, printers, and business software. The well-respected company name, Office Administration, was retained, but below the signs and the letterheads was written "Under New Management." The company began to prosper again. The company name and business were the same—Office Administration—but the product range was now suited to a new age and to the new ways that offices were run.

The story of the whole Bible is about Grace Administration. The New Testament tells us that the coming of Jesus changed the way grace is administered. The Old Testament administered the grace of Jesus in a way that suited the times and the people then—through prophecies, pictures, and symbols. It was glorious—for its time. But now, the same grace is to be administered directly and only through Jesus. Grace Administration is "Under New Management." As such, it is even more glorious:

"For if what is passing away was glorious, what remains is much more glorious."[2]

In other words, the New Testament is not a new business but a new way of administering the same business of grace. It is Grace Administration "Under New Management." It's not that the Old Testament was Law-Works Administration and the New Testament is Grace Administration. It's not a contrast of absolutes—law versus grace; it's a contrast of relatives—less grace versus more grace. The old management of Grace Administration was glorious, but the new management is far more glorious.

Lesser Grace versus Greater Grace

Does that illustration help you understand the contrast in John 1:17? This is not an absolute black-and-white contrast between law and grace, but a relative contrast between the lesser grace of the Old Testament era and the greater grace of the New Testament era. Significantly there is no middle "but" in the original Greek of John 1:17, an absence that helps tone down the impression of an absolute contrast.

Yet I'm not just basing this interpretation on a missing "but." Rodney Whitacre, professor of biblical studies, has pointed out, "The significant contrast in John is not of the law over against grace and truth, since it is the same graciousness of the same God that is revealed in both."[3] Whitacre instead finds the contrast in the verbs: the law *was given* (*edothe*); grace *came* (*egeneto*). Both verbs highlight divine graciousness, but the second intensifies and magnifies the first. The law was merely *given*. In Jesus, grace *came*:

So there is a contrast here, but it is one of degree. The grace received in Jesus is added upon the grace that came through Moses and the law. The association between the two is basically one of continuity, of the partial contrasted with the full. While there is continuity it is, nevertheless, a quantum leap that has occurred in Jesus, as verse 18 makes clear.[4]

The Puritan commentator Matthew Henry also speaks of the substitution of New Testament grace for Old Testament grace in verse 16 and goes on:

This sense is confirmed by what follows (v. 17); for the Old Testament had grace in type, the New Testament has grace in truth. There was a grace under the Old Testament, the gospel was preached then (Gal. 3:8); but that grace is superseded, and we have gospel grace instead of it, a glory which excels (2 Cor. 3:10). Discoveries of grace are now more clear, distributions of grace far more plentiful; this is grace instead of grace.[5]

Text in Context

This relative contrast view is supported first by the *wider biblical context*. The New Testament's view of the Old is not of contradiction but of completion and fulfillment. Jesus completed what the Old Testament could do only in part. We cannot say that Moses preached the opposite of Jesus because Moses spoke of Jesus. We cannot say that Israel had only the law, and we have the gospel: "For indeed the gospel was preached to us *as well as to them*."[6]

Second, there is the *context of the book* itself, in which we never find John disparaging the Old Testament.[7]

Third, the *context of the chapter* is enlightening. Several times in the first eighteen verses we see contrasts between less and greater, not between opposites. John the Baptist was a light but not the "*true* Light."[8] Jesus was "preferred before [John],"[9] but John's ministry was nevertheless owned by God. Therefore, the general argument seeks to exalt the preeminence of Jesus, not compared with what was contrary to His gospel but with what was of a lesser degree.

Finally there is the *immediate context*. The last words before verse 17 are "grace for grace" (NKJV), which could be translated "grace in addition to grace."[10] This addition of grace to grace is illustrated in verse 17, as confirmed by the linking word *for*. In other words, "grace in addition to grace" is demonstrated by God's supplementing the grace He revealed in the Old Testament with the superabounding grace of Christ's incarnation revealed in the New.

The consistent message of Christ and His apostles is that the Old Testament is all about Christ and His gracious salvation. Although there are passages in the New Testament that seem to contradict this, these seeming contradictions can be resolved by understanding them as critiques of the Old Testament as perverted by sinners or as comparisons of the lesser grace of the Old Testament with the greater grace of the New Testament.

Let's now pick up the gospel keys that Jesus and His apostles have provided for us and enjoy some blessed spiritual heartburn as we discover and enjoy Jesus on every page.[11]

PART 2

SPIRITUAL
HEARTBURN

CHAPTER 7

CHRIST'S PLANET

Discovering Jesus in the Creation

I used to think that Genesis 1–2 was all about evolution versus creation. I read lots of books, watched lots of DVDs, and listened to lots of sermons and lectures, all proving that God created the world in six twenty-four-hour days. I firmly believe that, but that's not the point. In fact, by majoring on that point, I missed the point altogether. After many years of debate and argument that were often far from the spirit of Jesus, I came to see that Genesis 1–2 is actually about Jesus. Yes, Jesus can be found and enjoyed even in the very opening chapters of the Old Testament. And if we grasp that, we should find these chapters generating a bit more light instead of the usual heat.

How did Genesis 1–2 change for me from being chapters full of debate to chapters full of Christ-centered devotion? As I had experienced previously, God forced me into it by forcing me to study it. A pastors' conference in Virginia asked me to speak on

Christ in creation. Thinking it would be a terribly short address, I wrote back and asked if I could add a few more chapters of Genesis so I would have a hope of speaking for more than one or two minutes. The organizers graciously granted permission.

STOPPED AND STUNNED

Early in my message preparation I read a verse that stopped me in my tracks: "By Him all things were created that are in heaven and that are on earth, visible and invisible, whether thrones or dominions or principalities or powers. *All things were created through Him and for Him.*"[1] I let that last sentence sink in. All things (not most things) were created (brought into existence) through Him (by the Son of God) and for Him (not for nothing and not for us but for Jesus). *Wow! There's enough here to preach ten messages*, I thought.

You might ask, as I did, what place does Christ have in the perfect world of Genesis 1–2? If there's no sin, surely there's no need of a Savior? Returning to one of my favorite books, Richard Pratt's *He Gave Us Stories*, I was reminded that although chapters 1 and 2 of Genesis describe a perfect world, they were originally written for Israel, a redeemed people in a fallen world. Although also written for us, these verses were written by Moses primarily to teach the newly redeemed people of Israel about their Redeemer God and to look to Him for an even greater Redeemer and redemption—a Redeemer greater than Moses and a redemption greater than a physical deliverance from Egyptian slavery.

That way of viewing Genesis as redemptive history is confirmed by the way the New Testament not only names Jesus as the Creator but also encourages us to view His creation in connection with His redemption, for example, John 1:1–3 and Hebrews 1:1–3. I concluded then that Genesis 1–2 is not so much about science, although it has nothing to fear from true science; it is about the person and work of Jesus. As I studied, I discovered several ways that these chapters reveal the Redeemer and His redemption.

THE ARRANGEMENT OF REDEMPTION

There was a plan of redemption before there was a creation.[2] Jesus the Redeemer was "the Lamb slain *from* the foundation of the world";[3] indeed, His saving work was "foreordained *before* the foundation of the world."[4] The Father, the Son, and the Holy Spirit had arranged to redeem the world before they created the world. They created the world with a view to redeeming it.

When we read the first chapter of Genesis, we must remember that not only the first lines and the first chapter but also the whole plan of redemption were already written. Redemption was already planned when God said, "Let there be light." Therefore we should view creation against the backdrop of the plan of redemption and as an integral part of it.

THE ARENA OF REDEMPTION

If the plan of redemption came before the creation, in Genesis 1–2 the Redeemer is creating the arena of His redemption. Jonathan Edwards, the New England pastor and theologian, wrote that this world "was doubtless created to be a stage upon which this great and wonderful work of redemption should be transacted."[5] When Jesus designed His world, He set the stage perfectly for the unfolding drama of redemption. He designed the props, the background, the lighting, the set, the actors, and so forth. He made sure that everything was suited to the redemption He planned to perform.

THE AIM OF REDEMPTION

The Bible describes Christian salvation using vocabulary from the original creation, indicating that one of the best ways to understand our salvation and our Savior is by studying the creation account. To put it another way, the Lord made Adam and Eve in such a way that the work of redemption and the Redeemer Himself would be better understood in the future.

For example, He made humanity in His own image,[6] an image that now has been damaged and defaced by sin. But notice how the New Testament describes Jesus as the perfect image of God,[7] and His work of redemption is presented as restoring the image of God in humanity.[8] Paul was saying, "If you want to understand who Jesus is and what He is doing in your redemption, go back to the original perfect image of God, Adam and Eve."

That's also why Jesus installed Adam as a prophet, a priest, and a king—to show us who the Redeemer is and how He redeems. As a prophet, Adam received God's word and commands for himself and his wife. As a priest, he served as a worshipping worker in the Lord's garden-temple. As a king, he ruled over the creation. Although Adam failed in these roles, Jesus came and filled these offices in a way Adam never did—and all to make His people prophets, priests, and kings again.[9]

We can understand this great Redeemer and His wonderful redemption so much better when we see the original model prophet, priest, and king in the garden of Eden.

THE ACCESSORIES OF REDEMPTION

Have you ever thought about the incredible imagination and inventiveness behind the created world and asked *why*? Why did our Redeemer go to such lengths to provide us with such a varied and diverse world? Partly the reason was that He had an eye to using these things, animals, materials, and so on to teach sinners the way of salvation. He was preparing visual aids for future use.

He created sheep so He could teach sinners about how He is the Good Shepherd.[10] He created birds to help His redeemed people live less anxious lives.[11] He created camels to teach how hard it is for those who trust in riches to enter heaven.[12] He created lilies and roses so He could compare Himself with them.[13] He created water to explain how He refreshes and revives the thirsty.[14]

When Jesus picked these up some four thousand years after their creation, they were not just coincidentally helpful to Him; He deliberately created them for the great end of helping to redeem a people.

And think of how Jesus even created what would be used in His own crucifixion. What did He think when He made the trees, one of which would one day suspend Him between heaven and earth? What did He think when He made the metal that would eventually impale Him on the cross? He made what would be used to cause Him pain and kill Him. He created all the accessories of redemption.

THE ASSISTANTS OF REDEMPTION

We're not told in Genesis 1–2 when the angels were created, but we know that they were created at some point in the six days. Why did Jesus create them? It wasn't because He as God needed them; He was not lonely and in need of company. It was because He knew that sinful men and women would need them. He created them to employ them as ministering spirits to the heirs of salvation.[15]

And although Jesus as God did not need the angels, He did need them as man. He made the angels that He knew would minister to His human needs after the wilderness temptations.[16] He made the angel that He knew would encourage Him in the desperate straits of Gethsemane.[17] When these angels came to Him, He knew them; He recognized them; He made them for this very purpose, to assist Him in His great work of redemption.

THE ADVANCE OF REDEMPTION

Much has been written about the order of creation. Why this order and not that? And many have pointed out how logical the order is. For example, the Lord did not create the fish and then the sea; He did not create animals and then their food; rather, it was the other way around. There are good, logical explanations for why the Lord advanced through the days of creation in the way He did. That kind of reasoning seems to forget that He could have created everything out of nothing in a moment. If He did not need to follow an order for physical reasons, why did He do it? He did it to illustrate how salvation advances and progresses.

For example, Moses was using the creation account to explain to Israel, the first readers of this book, how God redeemed them from Egypt and took them to the border of the promised land. He took them from virtual nonexistence in Egypt and gave them life. He took them from darkness to light. He found them formless and empty and shaped them and filled them as a nation. Genesis 1–2 gave Israel more insight into the kind of Redeemer that God was and what their redemption from Egypt was like.

There is much more here, however, than instruction for redeemed Israel. Jesus and his apostles used the creation theme to explain how God redeems our souls. Paul said that if any man is in Jesus, "he is a new creation."[18] Paul was saying, "If you want to find out what your salvation is like, go back to the creation account." And if we do, what do we find?

- Creation and salvation start with the life-giving Spirit.[19]
- Created life and salvation life begin with light.[20]
- Created light and salvation light separate from the darkness.[21]
- Creation and salvation produce fruit.[22]
- Creation and salvation move toward the climax of humanity in God's image.[23]
- Creation and salvation end with control and dominion.[24]

The Lord and His apostles used this creation order to illustrate how we experience salvation as it advances in the soul.

The Analogy of Redemption

Although Genesis 1–2 does not tell us that Adam was anything more than a single individual acting for himself, we can tell from the consequences of his sin that Adam was acting as "one for all."

The New Testament confirms that God created Adam as a representative man, a man representing the whole human race.[25] It also makes clear that Adam was created like this to illustrate how Jesus saves. Just as Adam was one man acting for many with such destructive consequences, so Jesus was one man acting for many with saving consequences.[26] We can understand the work of the Last Adam only by understanding the work of the First Adam.

The Advantages of Redemption

In Genesis 1–2, Jesus instituted the Sabbath and marriage with the redemptive purpose of highlighting the advantages of salvation. Although sin produces weariness and estrangement, redemption brings rest and relationship. The sabbath rest points forward to the rest of salvation and the rest of eternity.[27]

The marriage Christ performed in the garden of Eden was to later illustrate and explain the amazing marriage between Jesus and His church on earth and eventually in heaven too.[28] What wonderful benefits Jesus' redemption brings to us!

The Apex of Redemption

At least part of the eternal dwelling place of the redeemed was also created in Genesis 1–2. It is described as a "kingdom prepared . . .

from the foundation of the world."[29] Christ did not create heaven once salvation was seen to be necessary and He needed a place to put the people He redeemed. He created "all things," including the heavenly resting place of His redeemed, before there was any need for redemption.[30] What a moment when Abel, the first martyr, became the first believer to enter that place prepared for him from the foundation of the world!

THE AUTHOR OF REDEMPTION

I hope you now agree that Genesis 1–2 is about far more than creation versus evolution. It is ultimately about our redemption and our Redeemer. We approach these chapters not just with the question, what do they tell me about the world? and not just with, what do they tell me about God? but also with, what do they tell me about my Savior?

Creation tells us He is powerful. He willed into existence what previously had no existence. He made everything we see and everything we don't see. Throughout Genesis 1 we read, "Let it be . . ." and "it was so." Christ's supreme sovereignty is in the foreground. He is Lord of the creation, as He further demonstrated when He came to this earth: "Who can this be, that even the wind and the sea obey Him!"[31] Answer? The Creator of them.

The creation account also tells us that He is wise. We see order, progress, and development; we see divisions and distinction; we see regulation and rule. Nothing is accidental or coincidental; it is purposeful, always moving toward a goal.

Above all, creation communicates that He is good. The

creation was not dull and boring but full of invention, imagination, and variety. We see the goodness of Jesus in giving such a diverse, varied, and interesting world to humanity. We see His goodness in the abundance and the generosity.[32] We see His beauty in the Genesis 2 accounts of the environment. We see His goodness in His blessing of His work.[33] Several times we read: "And God saw that it was good." Everything about the creation says, "Jesus is gloriously good."

The Application of Redemption

Jesus made all the arrangements for redemption at the creation. He planned it. He designed the arena. He created humanity in such a way that we would better understand what we ought to be and can be through His work of new creation. He has furnished us with multiple visual aids that provide us with daily sermons. He has sent angels to serve those who are and who will be heirs of salvation. He designs the stages of redemption to illustrate and explain the way salvation progresses in the soul. He set up Adam as a representative man, who sadly chose death, so that we will grasp Jesus' representative work that brings life. He institutes marriage and the Sabbath to underline that salvation is about relationship and rest. He prepares a heavenly kingdom to house all His saved ones. He has done it all. He is so, so good.

Everything is prepared, and everything is ready. The stage of redemption is complete, the props are in place, the background is set, the music is playing, and the spotlight is on you. You are being called to redemption in Jesus. What are you doing? Are you running off the stage, rebelling against the reason for your existence? All things were made by Him and for Him. You were made for Him. Will you fulfill your role or be subject to stage fright? Realize the purpose of your creation by Him and for Him.

CHAPTER 8

CHRIST'S PEOPLE

*Discovering Jesus in the Old
Testament Characters*

Most of us use the Old Testament for moral examples, don't we? We turn there for heroes to inspire us and for villains to warn us. Joseph says, "Resist temptation!" Absalom says, "Don't be vain!" Nehemiah says, "Build the church!" Moses says, "Don't lose your temper!" I'm sure you've heard such sermons. Maybe you've preached them too. I certainly did. Is that the way God intended the Old Testament to be used? "Look at what he or she did and try to copy him or her. . . . And whatever you do, don't be like him or her." It sounds rather legalistic and moralistic, doesn't it?

When I started reading and teaching the Old Testament using the gospel keys provided by Christ and His apostles, I read books and listened to sermons that were highly critical of this biographical approach to the Old Testament. Although initially impressed by these critics, I eventually pulled back from them.

They were expressing valid concerns, yet I decided they were overreacting and going too far to the other side by rejecting any exemplary lessons from the Old Testament. Let's listen to some of their concerns and learn from them. Then I'll propose a way forward that I hope preserves the gospel story and its ethical impact on our story.

VALID CONCERNS

Here are the main criticisms of the biographical or "heroes and villains" approach to the Old Testament:

THE HEROES AND VILLAINS APPROACH IS MAN CENTERED

This approach changes the focus of God's Word from God to man. It tends to put man and his needs in the foreground with God and His glory in the background. For example, Haddon Robinson, professor of preaching, wrote, "God reveals himself in the Scriptures. The Bible, therefore, isn't a textbook about ethics or a manual on how to solve personal problems. The Bible is a book about God. When you study a biblical text, therefore, you should ask, 'What is the vision of God in this passage?' God is always there. Look for Him."[1] In the same vein he added: "The Bible is a book about God. It is not a religious book of advice about the 'answers' we need about a happy marriage, sex, work, or losing weight. Although the Scriptures reflect on many of those issues, they are above all about who God is and what God thinks and wills."[2]

Statistics seem to support the view that there are far too many man-centered sermons today. According to a study by *Preaching and Pulpit Digest*, "85% of sermons are anthropocentric. Most sermons are not grounded in the character, nature, and will of God."[3]

THE HEROES AND VILLAINS APPROACH IS MORALISTIC

It turns the Old Testament into a legalistic list of do's and don'ts or be's and don't be's. It focuses on what we should and shouldn't do rather than on what God has done and is doing.

THE HEROES AND VILLAINS APPROACH IS TOO FEELINGS BASED

We should read the text and understand it without trying to make subjective personal application. Indeed, such additions to the text are harmful because people seek assurance in introverted and discouraging self-examination: "I'm supposed to be brave like Daniel. But I'm not, so I can't be a Christian."

THE HEROES AND VILLAINS APPROACH FRAGMENTS THE BIBLE

It isolates the passage from the broad sweep of biblical history by focusing on small, individual atoms of Scripture rather than connecting them with the big picture. It's like looking at all the pieces of a puzzle individually, one after another—here's a theological bit, here's a moral bit, here's a historical bit, and so forth—instead of putting each piece in connection with the one united Word and work of God.

THE HEROES AND VILLAINS APPROACH IS CHRIST-LESS

When an Old Testament story is detached from the sweep of redemptive history, it often results in God-sermons but not Jesus-sermons. Some sermons, books, and Bible studies on Old Testament characters could easily have been taught by non-Christian religions.

The Heroes and Villains Approach Skips over the Original Meaning

We're such a self-centered bunch. It's often hard for us to read anything without first asking, what's in this for me? We find it difficult to think that God could have written the Old Testament for anyone but us. Actually He did. Although its message is also for us, it was primarily and originally for Israel. Instead of jumping straight from the text to us, we have to ask, what was the author's message for Israel?

The Heroes and Villains Approach Is Too Individualistic

It emphasizes individual personal piety to the exclusion of our corporate responsibility and of our relationship and responsibilities to the church and the state. It also tends to focus on my little life here on earth, with little emphasis on the future united life of God's people in the new heaven and new earth.

Sidney Greidanus calls us to "employ biblical characters the way the Bible employs them, not as ethical models, not as heroes for emulation or examples for warning, but as people whose story has been taken up into the Bible in order to reveal what *God* is doing for and through them."[4] Their personal history must be seen as part of the greater story of Israel's national history, which, in turn, is part of the even greater story of redemptive history.

Greidanus often uses David's battle with Goliath as an example of this approach. He says that although David certainly displayed exemplary courage in facing Goliath, the author of 1 Samuel was teaching Israel that their national security rested on God's anointed king alone.[5] And above all, the writer was teaching that David's victory was not the result of his relying on his own military skill; he was victorious because God fought for

Israel.[6] The personal and national battle is thereby transformed into a momentous chapter in the cosmic spiritual and redemptive battle that climaxes in Jesus' victory over Satan, initially at the cross and ultimately at Jesus' second coming, when He shall judge Satan and condemn him to the lake of fire and brimstone.[7]

OUR RESPONSE

How should we respond to these warnings? We can simply ignore all biographical chapters in the Bible. However, most of the Old Testament is biographical narrative, stories that open up fascinating and edifying windows into the struggles and successes of God's people. To ignore all this greatly impoverishes the church.

Alternatively we can use the biographies to teach us lessons about God and studiously avoid making any kind of personal application. However, the Bible uses the biographies to teach us how to believe and act. Paul highlighted how the Old Testament described Abraham's faith for our benefit.[8] In fact, later, Paul viewed the whole Old Testament as exemplary and the history of Israel in particular.[9] The apostle James pointed to Job and Elijah as examples for imitation.[10] The writer to the Hebrews held up Jesus and His Old Testament saints as examples.[11] The Lord Himself warned, "Remember Lot's wife."[12] In perhaps the briefest sentence he ever wrote, Dr. John Owen commented, "Old Testament examples are New Testament instructions."[13]

The best way forward is to listen carefully to the valid concerns expressed by biographical critics and modify our approach so that we can use these spiritual biographies in a more Christ-centered way. Our main aims must be to

- keep God, not man, in the foreground.
- distinguish Christian morality from mere moralism by realizing that we need Jesus' grace to obey any moral requirements and His forgiveness when we fail.
- avoid introspective subjectivism by looking away to Jesus far more than looking within for evidences of grace.
- relate every story to the overarching plan of redemption.
- look for Jesus when studying Jesus' people.
- find the original purpose for the original audience.
- include the corporate and eternal perspective even when looking at individual earthly lives.

Let me now describe numerous ways I found that can achieve these aims and yet still draw exemplary lessons from the Old Testament's biographies.

THE CONTROL OF JESUS

Because Jesus sovereignly controls everything and everybody, He arranged and ordered every Old Testament event and person.[14] Thus, even though every text does not name or refer to Jesus, He is implied in every text since the events and people of every text are part of His plan of redemption. Every story is connected with the overall story of salvation. Professor Bryan Chapell turned to the forest to illustrate:

> You do not explain what an acorn is, even if you say many true things about it (e.g., it is brown, has a cap, is found on the ground, is gathered by squirrels), if you do not in some

way relate it to an oak tree. In a similar sense, preachers cannot properly explain a seed (or portion) of biblical revelation, even if they say many true things about it, unless they relate it to the redeeming work of God that all Scripture ultimately purposes to disclose. In this sense, the entire Bible is Christ-centered because his redemptive work in all of its incarnational, atoning, rising, interceding, and reigning dimensions is the capstone of all of God's revelation of his dealings with his people. Thus, no aspect of revelation can be thoroughly understood or explained in isolation from some aspect of Christ's redeeming work.[14]

EXAMPLES: The faith of Abraham and the patience of Job point to the Jesus who arranged their personal providences and circumstances by His almighty sovereignty, as well as to the Jesus who worked faith and patience in their souls.[15]

THE CHARACTER OF JESUS

Any good accomplished by biblical characters was the work of the Spirit of Christ and reflected the formation of Jesus' image in them.[16] As such, these characters often point to Jesus by analogy—they are like Him—or they are witnesses to His character.

EXAMPLE: Joseph's forgiveness and acceptance of the brothers who had sinned against him reflect the spirit of Jesus who was in him. As such, Joseph is one of the most perfect analogies of Jesus' forgiving spirit and one of the most powerful witnesses to Jesus' forgiving heart.

THE CHURCH OF JESUS

The Old Testament was originally written for "the church in the wilderness."[17] That's why instead of jumping immediately to ask, what does this mean for me? we must pause and ask, what was the original message to the original readers of this Old Testament passage?

But how do we know what the original message was? We ask the main question that the Israelites asked when they read the Old Testament narratives. And what was that? The Old Testament was not primarily a history of Israel but a revelation of God—it revealed Him to Israel through their history. The first question the Israelites asked when they read the Old Testament was, what is God like?

In fact, we can be more specific. When Mr. and Mrs. Israelite read the Old Testament, they were asking, what is the coming Savior like? Jesus Himself said that if the people of Israel of His own day had properly searched the Old Testament Scriptures, they would have found Him, for they "testify of Me."[18]

And that testifying was not just with New Testament hindsight but with Old Testament foresight. The Old Testament was built upon a promise: a promise of a suffering and saving Messiah—a promise first given in Genesis 3:15; a promise that was expanded and clarified with every passing chapter and book; a promise that stimulated hope, expectation, and longing. As Jesus said, "Many prophets and righteous men desired to see what you see, and did not see it, and to hear what you hear, and did not hear it."[19]

Remember Peter taught us that although we understand more clearly than they did, the Old Testament prophets accurately predicted the saving sufferings of Jesus and the glory that would follow.[20] And just in case we think that maybe only a few later prophets grasped this, Peter assured us that God spoke of these things "by the mouth of *all* His holy prophets since the world began. . . . Yes, and *all* the prophets, from Samuel and those who follow, as many as have spoken, have also foretold these days."[21]

With that increasingly powerful forward momentum of Old Testament revelation, Mr. and Mrs. Israelite read the Old Testament and asked not only, what is God like? but also, what will the Messiah be like? What do we learn about the Savior from this book?

Moses himself provided this principle of interpretation by saying, "The LORD your God will raise up for you a Prophet like me from your midst."[22] Moses gave us the key question to ask when we read Exodus to Deuteronomy. And it's not so much, what was Moses like? That's a good start. But we must go beyond that by asking, what will the Messiah be like? These then are not primarily the books of Moses but more accurately the books of the Messiah.[23]

EXAMPLE: When we turn to the book of Ruth and ask this fundamental question—what is the coming Savior like?—our focus shifts radically from Ruth to Boaz. The book might equally be named after him because he is the center and pivot of the book. Chapter 1 begins with a bitter Naomi, and the book ends with a blessed Naomi. What made the difference? Three chapters of Boaz. All eyes should be on him.

The key word in the book also dramatically spotlights Boaz. The Hebrew word *ga'al* appears twelve times, and the noun version of it nine times.[24] It is variously translated, but it basically combines two elements: relation and redemption. It refers to a close family member who steps in to defend, protect, and provide for the needy. It's a word used to describe God's past action of redeeming Israel out of Egypt, and the later prophets also used it repeatedly to describe a future redemption that God would accomplish.

When Mr. and Mrs. Israelite were reading in Exodus about God's past redemption or in Isaiah about God's future redemption, they would perhaps turn to each other and ask, "Isn't there another book about redemption somewhere in the Scriptures? Oh, yes, that little book about Boaz has lots about redemption. Let's read there and find out about what kind of Redeemer God is and what kind of Redeemer the Messiah will be."

If you want to read Ruth like Mr. and Mrs. Israelite did, then ask, what is the Messiah like? And if you do, you will discover the beautiful answer: the Messiah is like Boaz. Notice Ruth's important genealogical postscript that further boosts the messianic momentum by tracing her descendants to King David.[25]

The Crimes Against Jesus

When Old Testament believers broke the law, they broke the law that was "ordained by angels in the hand of a mediator."[26] As that mediator was the Son of God, the laws they broke were His laws, and the penalties they suffered were His penalties—ordained and levied by Him.

Example: When David committed adultery and murder, he confessed, "Against You, You only, have I sinned, and done this evil in Your sight."[27] His crimes were all the harder for him to bear because he committed them against his Savior, the Son of God, the coming Messiah whom he loved and trusted.

THE CONTRAST WITH JESUS

Due to the sins and shortcomings of the Old Testament believers, we can often discover Jesus from their lives by way of contrast. Whereas they failed, He succeeded; whereas they gave up, He persevered; whereas they were defeated by evil, He conquered it. What a beautiful contrast Jesus is to even the best of His people!

EXAMPLE: The repeated failures of the Israelites to overcome temptation in the wilderness may be contrasted with Jesus' emphatic victory over temptation in the same wilderness.[28]

THE CALL FOR JESUS

The sins of Bible characters reveal how much they needed a Savior and induce a cry for Him. If there is one thing the Old Testament calls for, it is that God would come and fully redeem His people. In multiple texts we are confronted with the fallen condition of humanity and our need of a Savior.

EXAMPLE: The last book to be written in the Old Testament was not Malachi but Nehemiah. And what a disappointing note it ends on! The earlier obedience and celebration of 12:27—13:3 contrast starkly with the final failures in 13:4–31. Although the Ezra-Nehemiah period began with high hopes, it ended with spiritual failure. Restored Israel rebuilt the city, but the spiritual rebuilding was weak and fragile. Time and again Nehemiah prayed, "Remember me, O my God."[29] The whole scene called out for something more, for the power and grace of a successful Savior.

The Confession to Jesus

By offering sacrifices, the Israelites were taught what their sins deserved—death. It is a common misconception that the animal sacrifices saved them from sin. However, the New Testament is crystal clear: the blood of bulls and goats could never take away sin.[30] Instead, the sacrifices reminded and convicted them of sin.[31] That's why they had to be brought with a contrite and broken spirit.[32]

Although the sacrifices did not cleanse or pacify the conscience, they did purify the flesh;[33] they gave a ceremonial "forgiveness" that allowed *physical* proximity between the offerer and God's presence in the tabernacle and temple. But of themselves the sacrifices had no impact on *spiritual* proximity to God. As one of the Reformers said,

> For what is more vain or absurd than for men to offer a loathsome stench from the fat of cattle in order to reconcile themselves to God? Or to have recourse to the sprinkling of water and blood to cleanse away their filth? In short, the whole cultus of the law, taken literally and not as shadows and figures corresponding to the truth, will be utterly ridiculous . . . if the forms of the law be separated from its end, one must condemn it as vanity.[34]

No spiritually minded Israelite ever imagined that an animal sacrifice could form the basis of his salvation. Rather, it made him long in faith for a better and greater sacrifice that would.

Because Israel's sacrifices had to be offered via a priest, they reminded the people of their need for a mediator to go between them and God. And again the very imperfection of even the best human mediator reminded the people of their need of a far better, a perfect, mediator.

EXAMPLES: David confessed that sacrifices alone were not enough but had to be brought with a humble spirit.[35] No one was given a clearer picture of the future sacrifice that would save than Isaiah.[36] Job confessed his need for a mediator or an umpire between himself and God, and at times he testified that he was already looking toward such a mediating Redeemer.[37]

THE COMPASSION OF JESUS

Jesus' mercy and compassion are not limited to the New Testament. Just as we see Him saving the unworthy in the New Testament, we see Him doing the same in the Old Testament. Knowing that He would later suffer, die, and rise again to purchase redemption for sinners, He applied the benefits of that future redeeming work before it actually took place.

EXAMPLES: What mercy for Jesus to save David! What compassion for Jesus to save Samson! What forgiveness for Jesus to pardon Rahab the harlot![38]

CONVERSION TO JESUS

Whenever we read of souls being converted in the Old Testament, it is to the Messiah they were turned—not to God in general, but to Christ in particular. They heard the gospel, and they believed in the coming Savior.[39] Unless we understand that sinners in the Old and New Testaments were only saved by grace through faith in the Messiah, we will view the old covenant believers as moralists, ritualists, and legalists; sermons about them will also be moralistic, ritualistic, and legalistic.

If New Testament believers are going to sit down at the same heavenly table as Abraham, Isaac, and Jacob, then we must assume that we all get there the same way.[40] There cannot be some who got there by grace through faith in Jesus and others who got there by works through animal sacrifices. Otherwise some are going to be praising Jesus while others are going to be polishing their own halos. Doesn't sound like a very good recipe for fellowship.

EXAMPLE: Consider how Jacob was transformed from a manipulative schemer to a humble saint who looked forward to the coming King.[41] Who else could accomplish this change but Jesus? The Westminster Confession of Faith, one of the church's summaries of the Bible's teaching, explains how Jesus could save sinners who lived and died before the incarnation:

> Although the work of redemption was not actually wrought by Christ till after His incarnation, yet the virtue, efficacy, and benefits thereof were communicated unto the elect, in all ages successively from the beginning of the world, in and by those promises, types, and sacrifices, wherein He was revealed.[42]

CONFIDENCE IN JESUS

The Hebrews 11 examples of Old Testament faith come after ten chapters setting forth Jesus in the Old Testament institutions and ceremonies; we are clearly being asked to see their faith as Christ centered. Old Testament faith was Christ-centered faith.[43] Of course, Old Testament faith was shadow faith, but shadow implies at least some light. They did not see as much as New Testament Christians, they did not have as much of the Holy Spirit, and they did not have as strong assurance of the Father's love, but they had at least shadow versions of them.

But what did these Old Testament believers believe about Jesus? There were three main emphases to their faith: the Messiah will be a man, the Messiah will suffer, and the Messiah will conquer. All three truths appear in seed form in the first gospel promise in Genesis 3:15, where we are told that (1) the Messiah will be a man from the seed of the woman; (2) the Messiah will suffer as the Devil bruises His heel; and (3) the Messiah will conquer as He crushes the Devil's head. These three gospel seeds are developed, unfolded, and expanded throughout the Old Testament.

Sometimes one truth accelerates ahead of the others. For example, the seed of the woman is most prominent in the promises to Abraham in Genesis 12, 15, and 17; the Messiah's sufferings are prominent in the sacrificial system established in Exodus and Leviticus; the hopes of the Messiah's kingly triumph are inflated with the establishment of David's monarchy. Also, at times, the political situation accented one of these truths in the lives of the believers. For example, the painful Roman occupation of Israel made many believers, even the disciples, focus almost exclusively on the conquering Messiah emphasis.

But however imbalanced their faith may have become at times, Old Testament believers had conscious faith in the coming Christ. Pastor and author Charles Drew cited Hebrew 11:1—12:2 and commented, "Their faith points us to Jesus, and it does so in at least three ways: he is the object of their faith, he is the perfect model of their imperfect faith, and he is the builder of their faith."[44]

EXAMPLE: In John 5:45–47, Jesus told the Jews of His day that Moses, their great hero, would one day accuse them of failing to understand the Christ-centered meaning of the books he wrote. As professor of Jewish Studies Michael Rydelnik says, "Moses had to understand that he wrote of Messiah in the Torah or he would not be qualified to accuse those who did not correctly interpret the messianic hope in the Torah."[45]

Charles Drew explained the significant limitations but also the clear Christ-centered focus of Old Testament faith:

> Did Moses know the human name of Christ? No. Did Abraham know in detail how the heavenly country would be won for him? No. But their limited knowledge did not keep them from looking to the same Savior in whom we trust. Jesus Christ has always been the hope of his people, whether they have known his name or not. Abel, Enoch, Noah, Sarah, Joseph, Rahab, Gideon, and so many more all looked to Jesus Christ, for they "all died in faith," looking to the promises of God, the promises whose final "yes" is in Jesus Christ.[46]

THE COPY OF JESUS

While we want to connect each Old Testament biography with the grand narrative of redemption, we must also preserve the moral application for the individual, for the church, and for society, all within a gospel framework. In *The Ancient Love Song*, Pastor Charles Drew noted how Old Testament saints are imperfect models of the life of faith that we find perfectly in Jesus Christ. From their lives we can learn something of what it meant for Jesus to live the life of faith in this world. He went on, "Their faithfulness anticipates the perfect faithfulness of the great Savior, who is their (and our) substitute, not only in his death, but also in the way that he lived."[47]

EXAMPLES: When Abraham offered up Isaac believing that God was able to raise him from the dead, he was mirroring, though imperfectly, the great confidence of Jesus when offering up His life.[48]

When Joseph forgave his brothers, he was picturing the future work of Jesus, which even then was working in Joseph, by the Spirit of Jesus. Used in this way, the Old Testament characters should motivate worship and imitation of Jesus.

THE COMMAND OF JESUS

Old Testament saints were often given leadership roles; they were ordained to command and captain God's people. Whenever they faithfully performed this role, they were portraying and predicting the same leadership role that Jesus would one day publicly fill.

EXAMPLES: Consider the courageous yet compassionate leadership of Elijah and Elisha who so faithfully portrayed the Lord who had called them, and predicted the Lord who would one day succeed and excel them in leading the charge against evil and in inspiring godly living.

THE CROSS OF JESUS

Many Old Testament saints were called to an experience of leadership that was associated with suffering. This repeated pattern of righteous and innocent suffering in leadership prefigured the suffering of Jesus and made Old Testament believers long for One who would not only put things right but also show the purpose of the pain.

EXAMPLES: Moses, Joshua, and Samuel are good examples. But the preeminent example is David who, despite being God's anointed, suffered at the hands of Saul, Ahithophel, and Absalom. It's no coincidence that Christ uses the exact words of David's laments to articulate His own sufferings.

THE CALL OF JESUS

As with all Scripture, Jesus calls us through the lives of Old Testament saints. He calls us to learn from them and follow Him. Though Jesus may not be mentioned specifically, behind every word are the mind of Jesus and the salvation of Jesus. Jesus is everywhere in the Old Testament, but He is everywhere in different ways.

EXAMPLE: One of the greatest fallacies about Old Testament saints is that they were focused on earthly cities, earthly treasures, and earthly rewards. But in Hebrews 11:9–10, 13–16, Jesus calls us to follow their example of looking for a heavenly city, heavenly treasures, and heavenly rewards. Their understanding and embrace of the gospel promises transformed this earth into a foreign land in which they felt like strangers, pilgrims, and aliens. However, their faith also transformed heaven into the Fatherland (literal translation of "homeland" in v. 14). The seventh Article of the Church of England, another classical summary of the Christian faith, puts it like this:

The Old Testament is not contrary to the New: for both in the Old and New Testament everlasting life is offered to Mankind by Christ, who is the only Mediator between God and Man, being both God and Man. Wherefore they are not to be heard, which feign [imagine] that the old Fathers did look only for transitory promises.[49]

The Crowning of Jesus

Another way of seeing Jesus in the lives of Bible characters is by considering how He was glorified by their lives on earth—by their praises of Him and by others praising Him for them. And these Old Testament believers now glorify Jesus in heaven. Let's lift up our eyes above this world and this scene of time to the heavenly realm, to the church of the firstborn, and both "see and hear" Old Testament saints there.[50]

EXAMPLES: Who can resist praising Jesus for the courageous life of Daniel, the purity of Joseph, the loyalty of Ruth, and so forth? Who can resist praising Jesus when we hear the submissive words of Job, the wise words of Solomon, and the worshipping words of David?

Who can resist praising Jesus when we think about heaven, when we come in our thoughts to "mount Sion, and unto the city of the living God, the heavenly Jerusalem, and to an innumerable company of angels, to the general assembly and church of the firstborn, which are written in heaven, and to God the Judge of all, and to the spirits of just men made perfect"?[51]

Crown Him! Crown Him! Crown Him! Crown Him Lord of all.

CHAPTER 9

CHRIST'S PRESENCE

*Discovering Jesus in His Old
Testament Appearances*

When a famous author dies, his or her relatives may find unpublished material among the files. The family often publishes these works posthumously, and mourning fans who had resigned themselves to never again reading a new word from their hero's pen rush to buy this bonus material.

Most Christians delight in reading and rereading the record of Jesus contained in the four Gospels. These four short books reveal so much about our precious Savior. But what would you say if I told you that I knew of some bonus material about Him? What if I told you there were other books—books that most people know very little about? No, I'm not talking about some newly discovered Gnostic gospels. In fact, the books I'm talking about were written hundreds of years before a star appeared in the east.

You won't be surprised to learn that I'm talking about the Old Testament. Yes, the Son of God was present and active on earth long before His birth in Bethlehem. This was probably my most exciting discovery when I started looking for Jesus in the Old Testament. Numerous writers, including Jonathan Edwards and Jonathan Stephens, opened my eyes to see the amount of bonus material that I had completely overlooked till then.[1]

I'm not quite sure what I used to think Christ was doing during the four thousand years of Old Testament history. Was He just idling His time away while waiting for His incarnation? Or maybe vexing His heart as He watched even the best of sinners destroy themselves through ill-fated attempts to please God with law keeping and sacrifice offering? Or perhaps He was merely spectating silently on the sidelines as His Father worked away on His own for four millennia? None of that made sense.

What did make sense was that the Son of God not only was busy in heaven during these four thousand years but also frequently visited the earth and appeared to His people in different forms, primarily as the Angel of the Lord and as the Glory of the Lord. We're going to survey this bonus material, but first, let's get a grip on some important biblical truths to help us better understand these wonderful pre-Bethlehem visits of Christ to the earth.

THE SON OF GOD IS THE ETERNAL SON OF GOD

As the second person of the Godhead, equal in power and glory with the Father and the Holy Spirit, the Son of God is identified with all of God's purposes, messages, and actions. But the Son also had unique functions and roles in the creation of the world[2] and in holding together and managing that creation afterward.[3]

He not only existed but was executing important tasks prior to His coming to this world in the flesh.

The Son of God Is the Usual Way God Speaks to Humanity

John called Jesus the eternal Word because God speaks to sinners only through the channel of His Son, in both the Old and the New Testaments.[4] One of the Reformers said that God never spoke directly to mankind but only and ever through His Son:

> Holy men of old knew God only by beholding him in his Son as in a mirror (cf. 2 Cor. 3:18). When I say this, I mean that God has never manifested himself to men in any other way than through the Son, that is, his sole wisdom, light, and truth. From this fountain Adam, Noah, Abraham, Isaac, Jacob, and others drank all that they had of heavenly teaching. From the same fountain, all the prophets have also drawn every heavenly oracle that they have given forth.[5]

Although He sometimes used prophets as His mouthpiece, the Son of God was always the ultimate Speaker. What about Jesus' baptism and transfiguration, though? Do we not hear the Father and see the Spirit there? These unique and unprecedented redemptive events are rare exceptions to the rule of God's usual way of working. They were necessary because of the people's—and even the disciples'—failure to recognize that this seemingly quite ordinary person was the image of the invisible God. Thus the need for the Father to publicly acknowledge His Son and command, "Hear Him!"

The Old Testament, then, is as much Jesus' message to us as the New Testament. As the apostle John wrote: "The testimony of Jesus is the spirit of prophecy."[6]

THE SON OF GOD IS THE USUAL WAY
GOD APPEARS TO HUMANITY

Just as the Son of God is the usual way God *speaks* to humanity, so also the Son of God is the usual way God *appears* to humanity: "No one has seen God at any time. The only begotten Son, who is in the bosom of the Father, He has declared Him."[7] Not only was the Son the audible voice of God, but He was also the visible face of God. He is the way Moses saw "Him who is invisible."[8] Jonathan Edwards explained:

> When we read in sacred history what God did from time to time towards his church and people, and what he said to them, and how he revealed himself to them, we are to understand it especially of the second Person of the Trinity. When we read of God's appearing after the Fall, from time to time, in some visible form or outward symbol of his presence, we are ordinarily, if not universally, to understand it of the second Person of the Trinity.[9]

The early church father Tertullian put it like this:

> It was the Son who judged men from the beginning, destroying that lofty tower, and confounding their languages, punishing the whole world with a flood of waters, and raining fire

and brimstone upon Sodom and Gomorrah . . . for he always descended to hold converse with men, from Adam even to the patriarchs and prophets, in visions, in dreams, in mirrors, in dark sentences, always preparing his way from the beginning: neither was it possible, that God who conversed with men upon earth, could be any other than that Word which was to be made flesh.[10]

The Son of God Is the Angel of the Lord

The term *Angel of the Lord* occurs more than fifty times in the Old Testament, and *Angel of God* occurs nine times. *Angel* means "messenger," a word that describes an angel's function rather than what an angel was made of; angels are God's messengers sent to serve the heirs of salvation.[11] A special Angel appears from time to time in the Old Testament, an Angel who is given divine titles, performs divine functions, and accepts divine worship. He is the Son of God, God's special messenger for special people at special times. Malachi, who used messenger language to predict the coming of the incarnate Jesus, confirmed this:

> "Behold, I send My messenger,
> And he will prepare the way before Me.
> And the Lord, whom you seek,
> Will suddenly come to His temple,
> Even the Messenger [lit. Angel] of the covenant,
> In whom you delight.
> Behold, He is coming,"
> Says the LORD of hosts.[12]

This coming Lord, this "Messenger [Angel] of the covenant" was the Son of God. He was sent to reveal God and can equally say with the incarnate Jesus, "He who has seen Me has seen the Father."[13] He, too, is the "brightness of [the Father's] glory and the express image of His person."[16]

To prove that this Angel of the Lord was the Son of God, we need only prove the Angel's deity. If the Angel was God, He was the Son of God, for as we have seen above, God was made audible or visible only through the Son of God. Here are six proofs of this Angel's deity:

1. *He claims divine authority.* He speaks as only God can and swears by Himself as only God can.[15]

2. *He is a distinct divine person.* At times He is identified with Jehovah; at other times He is carefully distinguished, highlighting the distinct individual persons of the Godhead.[16]

3. *He exhibits divine attributes.* For example, Hagar realized that this Angel had an omniscient awareness of her personal circumstances: her name, occupation, and location.[17] He also knew her current status of being pregnant and the gender of the child, and He even directed the selection of the child's name.[18] No wonder she described Him as "the-God-Who-Sees."[19]

4. *He performs divine actions.* He utters curses of divine judgment, judges, and redeems sinners.[20]

5. *He receives divine homage.* The Angel is to be treated as God.[21] He receives sacrifice from Gideon and is called Jehovah-Shalom, "The Lord-Is-Peace."[22]

6. *He is identified as God.* The literal translation of Hagar's

words in Genesis 16:13 is: "Then she called [the] name of the LORD, the One speaking to her, 'You [are the] God of appearance,' for she said, 'Have even I seen here the One who sees me?'" In Genesis 22, the Angel of the Lord and the Lord are spoken of as one and the same person.[23] In Genesis 31, the Angel identifies Himself as God: "Then the Angel of God spoke to me in a dream, saying, 'Jacob . . . I am the God of Bethel.'"[24] After speaking with the Angel, Samson's father, Manoah, exclaimed to his wife: "We shall surely die, because we have seen God!"[25]

God says of this Angel, "My name is in Him,"[26] which means that God's character is revealed in Him. Charles Hodge points out the uniqueness of this Angel:

> If this were a casual matter, if in one or two instances the messenger spoke in the name of him who sent him, we might assume that the person thus designated was an ordinary angel or minister of God. But when this is a pervading representation of the Bible; when we find that these terms are applied, not first to one, and then to another angel indiscriminately, but to one particular angel; that the person so designated is also called the Son of God, the Mighty God; that the work attributed to him is elsewhere attributed to God himself; and that in the New Testament, this manifested Jehovah, who led his people under the Old Testament economy, is declared to be the Son of God, the λογος, who was manifested in the flesh, it becomes certain that by the angel of Jehovah in the early books of Scripture, we are to understand a divine person, distinct from the Father.[27]

In summary, because this Angel is God and God reveals Himself through His Son, we must conclude that this Angel is the Son of God in human form. And I emphasize human *form*. He appeared in human *form* in the Old Testament but did not actually become human *flesh* until the New Testament.

APPEARANCES AS THE ANGEL OF THE LORD

With these biblical principles in hand, let us now draw some lessons from the Old Testament appearances of the Son of God. We will consider, first, the Angel of the Lord appearances, then the Glory of the Lord appearances.

THE APPEARANCES COMMUNICATE GRACE

Whether it's pregnant Hagar dying in the desert, fearful Gideon anticipating genocide at the hands of the Midianites, Abraham with a knife poised above his son, or Jacob expecting death at the hand of Esau, the Son of God sees their needs and comes as the Angel of the Lord with messages and actions full of grace and truth.

THE APPEARANCES REVEAL CONSTANT ACTIVITY

As the Angel of the Lord, Christ was continually at work throughout the Old Testament—revealing, redeeming, covenanting, interceding, protecting, comforting, commissioning, and judging.[28] Theologian John Walvoord summed it up:

> The combined testimony of these passages portrays the Son of God as exceedingly active in the Old Testament, dealing with sin, providing for those in need, guiding in the path of the will of

God, protecting His people from their enemies and, in general, executing the providence of God. The references make plain that this ministry is not occasional or exceptional but rather the common and continual ministry of God to His people. The revelation of the person of the Son of God thus afforded is in complete harmony with the New Testament revelation.[29]

According to professor of theology Anthony Hanson, the New Testament writers' central affirmation "is that the pre-existent Jesus was present in much of Old Testament history, and that therefore it is not a question of tracing types in the Old Testament for New Testament events, but rather of tracing the activity of the same Jesus in the old and new dispensations."[30]

The Appearances Diminish as the Word Increases

The appearances of the Son as the Angel of the Lord are especially prominent in the early part of the Old Testament and then gradually diminish with the passage of time. Why? It's partly because as revelations of the written Word increased, revelations of the preincarnate Word were less necessary. But the rarer and rarer appearances also created a growing longing in God's people for a fuller and longer-lasting revelation of the Son on earth. And that brings us to our next lesson.

The Appearances Prepare the Church for Jesus

Charles Drew illustrated how these appearances of the Son aroused love and longing in His people's hearts:

Lovers cannot bear to be apart. Phone calls and long letters do not satisfy the longing to be together; they only intensify it. The Old Testament appearances of the eternal Son are like those phone calls and letters. They are temporary, incomplete, and distant, designed to awaken in us a longing for God's permanent, intimate, full, and gracious appearing in the Incarnation.[31]

The Appearances Prepare Christ for His Saving Work

As well as preparing the church and giving believers a foretaste of the Messiah's mission, these visits prepared Christ and gave Him a foretaste of His messianic mission.[32] He had a foretaste of His prophetic ministry by delivering God's messages to needy humanity.[33] He had a foretaste of His priestly ministry by His glorious presence in the tabernacle and by His ascending to heaven in the flames of Manoah's sacrifice.[34] He had a foretaste of His kingly ministry by judging the heathen and by leading and ruling His people.[35] How much Christ longed to fully take up His roles of prophet, priest, and king of His people!

The Old Testament appearances of Christ in human form have been portrayed as expressions of holy impatience. They give an insight into His earnest desire to be involved with the sons of men. As the old Christians in the Scottish Highlands used to say to me, "Christ enjoyed trying on the clothes of His incarnation." What delicious appetizers of His great gospel work when He would no longer be simply God manifest in human *form* but God manifest in human *flesh*.

Appearances as the Glory of the Lord

In addition to appearing as a Messenger in human form, the Son of God appeared to Old Testament believers in the form of fire and smoke. This awesome fiery cloud, or cloudy fire, is usually called the Glory of the Lord.

In Exodus 3, we read that the Angel of the Lord appeared to Moses "in a flame of fire from the midst of a bush" (v. 2). This particular incident is also referred to in Deuteronomy 33:16, which speaks of "the good will of him that dwelt in the bush" (KJV). By putting together Exodus 3 and Deuteronomy 33, we can say that the Angel of the Lord, who is the Son of God, inhabited or occupied the fiery Glory of the Lord in the burning bush.

What do these appearances as the Glory-cloud of God teach us about the Son of God?

HE LEADS

Moses said that the Lord was the Angel of God who went before Israel to lead them and behind to protect them, and that He did so in the pillar of cloud by day, which in the dark glowed like a pillar of fire.[36]

HE DEFENDS

Exodus 14:19 teaches us that the Angel who dwelt in the pillar of cloud and fire also went behind Israel to protect them. This guarding ministry is confirmed by Exodus 23:20–23.

> Behold, I send an Angel before you to keep you in the way and to bring you into the place which I have prepared. Beware of Him and obey His voice; do not provoke Him, for He will not pardon your transgressions; for my name is in Him. But if you indeed obey His voice and do all that I speak, then I will be an enemy to your enemies and an adversary to your adversaries. For my Angel will go before you and bring you in to the Amorites.[37]

In 1 Corinthians 10:1–4, Paul identified this cloudy presence as Christ and said that His spiritual presence was spiritual food and drink to the Israelites.

He Communes

When Moses sprinkled the blood of the covenant on the people, the Son of God revealed Himself through the Glory-cloud to Moses and others. They "saw the God of Israel," and yet they all ate and drank together in sweet fellowship.[38]

He Speaks

The Lord descended to the tabernacle in the Glory-cloud and "spoke to Moses face to face, as a man speaks to his friend."[39]

He Sympathizes

This same Glory-inhabiting Son of God is also described as the presence of Jehovah,[40] a divine presence who was "touched with the feeling of our infirmities."[41]

So He became their Savior.
In all their affliction He was afflicted,
And the Angel of His Presence saved them;
In His love and in His pity He redeemed them;
And He bore them and carried them
All the days of old.[42]

He Commands

The law was given in the midst of awesome cloud and fire displays of the Glory of the Lord.[43] Stephen explained that Moses "was in the congregation in the wilderness with the Angel who spoke to him on Mount Sinai, and with our fathers, the one who received the living oracles to give to us."[44]

He Anticipates

The Glory-cloud also filled the tabernacle from time to time, anticipating His future tabernacling "among us" in the flesh.[45] The Glory-cloud especially occupied the space between the cherubim in the Most Holy Place of the tabernacle and the temple. God said, "I will appear in the cloud above the mercy seat."[46] And when He did, as the Son of God, He witnessed the high priest's annual sprinkling of the mercy seat with atoning blood, anticipating the giving of His own lifeblood for sinners.

He Reveals

When Moses prayed, "Please, show me Your glory," the Son of God "descended in the cloud and stood with him there, and proclaimed the name of the Lord."[47]

When on this earth, Jesus was again surrounded with the Glory-cloud at His transfiguration.[48] That was probably what John was referring to when he wrote, "The Word became flesh and dwelt among us, *and we beheld His glory*, the glory as of the only begotten of the Father, full of grace and truth."[49] He ascended to heaven in the same glorious cloud-chariot. And one day, in "like manner" He will return in the Glory-cloud, "and every eye shall see him."[50] As it was in the Old and New Testaments, so the last day will be gloriously cloudy!

CHAPTER 10

CHRIST'S PRECEPTS

Discovering Jesus in the Old Testament Law

The land of the free has a lot of laws. In addition to federal laws at a national level, each state has its own laws, and even within individual states, different cities often have different bylaws. Obviously, it's very important to know which law applies where. If I'm texting while driving in Ohio, I'd better be sure to stop before I cross the border into Michigan where it is now illegal. If someone wants to propose or challenge a law, he needs to know whether to write to Washington or approach his state legislature. In various ways we learn how to distinguish and recognize how different laws apply, or we suffer loss.

Similarly, if we fail to distinguish between different kinds of Old Testament law, we will suffer great spiritual loss. That's why I begin this chapter by identifying three types of Old Testament law—moral, ceremonial, and civil—and how Jesus fulfills all of them but in different ways.[1] Then I want to show you how Jesus

reveals Himself even in the Bible's laws; they are Jesus' precepts—
they are from Him and about Him.

THREE KINDS OF LAW

1. MORAL LAW

God gave His moral law to our first parents, Adam and Eve.
Although they rejected God's law by sinning, traces of it remain
imprinted on every human conscience.[2] God also gave a summary of the moral law at Mount Sinai. Although it was given first
to the nation of Israel, and some of its applications were specific
to Israel, the ten basic moral principles were to be a permanent moral code for all people at all times. As the Westminster
Confession of Faith puts it: "The moral law doth forever bind all,
as well justified persons as others, to the obedience thereof."[3]

2. CEREMONIAL LAW

The ceremonial law guided the Israelites in their tabernacle
and temple worship. Although permanent moral principles and
duties were revealed in the ceremonial laws (for example, the
principle of holy worship and the duty of preparing for worship
by holy living), the actual ceremonies themselves were abolished
when Jesus replaced the tabernacle and the temple with Himself.[4]
Again, the Westminster Confession explains:

> Besides this law, commonly called moral, God was pleased to
> give to the people of Israel, as a Church under age, ceremonial
> laws, containing several typical ordinances, partly of wor-
> ship, prefiguring Christ, His graces, actions, sufferings, and

benefits; and partly, holding forth divers instructions of moral duties. All which ceremonial laws are now abrogated, under the New Testament.[5]

3. CIVIL LAW

The civil law contained precepts and penalties that governed Israel's society. Many of these laws were given to protect and preserve Israel from threats to its existence, both from within and from without, until the Messiah came forth from it. But when the Messiah came and Israel rejected Him, God sent the Romans in AD 70 to sweep Israel away—together with its special civil laws. However, the general principles of justice underlying these laws should still be studied and applied in appropriate ways in our own day. Speaking of Old Testament Israel, the Westminster Confession states, "To them also, as a body politic, He gave sundry judicial laws, which expired together with the state of that people; not obliging any other now, further than the general equity thereof may require."[6]

LAW VERSUS GOSPEL?

With these foundational distinctions in place, let's look at ten ways in which Jesus' laws reveal Him. This idea is probably a bit alien to you. How can the law reveal Jesus? Surely the law is the enemy of Jesus and of us all? Have we not often heard the law contrasted with the gospel? How can it therefore show us Jesus and the gospel?

I understand your skepticism; I used to share it. That is, until I read *The Shadow of Christ in the Law of Moses* by Vern Poythress, a title that neatly sums up the way that we find Jesus even in the law. He's not center stage in the spotlights, but He's there in the shadows. He's there if you look closely and thoughtfully at the whole scene. Let me take you on a brief tour and show you Jesus in the law.

An Exhibition of Christ's Character

A person's words tell us much about him. This is especially true of God. Because all His words are perfectly free of deceit, hypocrisy, or pretense, they are perfectly self-revealing. They tell us who He is. And the fact that so much of God's Word, especially the early part, is taken up with law tells us a lot about God's character. Christopher Wright said, "Before we preach law to people, we need to make sure they know the God who stands behind it and the story that goes before it. It is the God of grace and the story of grace."[7]

As Jesus is God's eternal Word,[8] who equally with the Father and the Spirit inspired God's written Word,[9] and also became God's enfleshed Word, the law reveals the Son's character as well as the Father's and the Spirit's. In fact, the New Testament ties Jesus even closer to the law by saying that the Son was the Messenger who gave the law to Moses on Mount Sinai.[10] What does the law reveal about its Giver?

Jesus Is Sovereign

The Old Testament precepts communicate the sovereign authority of the divine Lawgiver through the awesome signs and wonders that accompanied the giving of the law at Sinai, and through the unambiguous and undebatable manner of their framing. "Thou shalt" and "Thou shalt not" leave no room for debate, adjustment, or compromise.

Jesus Is Holy

The spotless and beautiful ethics of the moral law, the laws of cleanliness and separation in the ceremonial law, and the separation of Israel from other nations through the civil law—all reveal the holy character of Christ, the perfect Israel of God, as "holy, harmless, undefiled, separate from sinners."[11]

Jesus Is Just

In the moral law we see Christ's concern for fairness and equity between God and man, and between man and man. In the penalties attached to the civil law we see that Christ does not just give the law and then show little interest in whether it is kept or not. Rather, the penalties show His passion for justice and redress.

Jesus Is Wise

The law of God reveals the wisdom of Christ. No nation has abandoned the wisdom of God expressed in the moral law and prospered. The general principles and much of the practice of the civil law have underpinned the most successful countries, empires, and civilizations in world history.

Jesus Is Good

God's giving of the law to Israel was an expression of His favor and goodness toward them.[12] Never was any nation so privileged as to have such laws. If the nation practiced these laws, the nation's existence and prosperity would be secured.[13] The moral law shows the Lord's benevolent interest in every single area of human life: worship, speech, family life, business, poverty, oppression, and so forth.

Jesus Is Savior

The moral and civil law addressed and sought to reverse the irregularity and disorder brought about by sin. It therefore had a restorative or redemptive purpose. It showed the Lord's desire to restore order and regularity to His world and to redeem it from its fallen state. The ceremonial laws of cleanness and uncleanness reveal not only God's concern about uncleanness but also His willingness and ability to wash it away and restore the defiled person to life and communion with Him.

In summary, the law predicts God's intention to restore order to His world, to cleanse it from defilement, and to restore its inhabitants to communion with Him. In so doing, it reveals Christ's beautiful character.

An Exposition of Jesus' Life

The law exhibits the preincarnate character of the eternal Son of God, and it also expounds His incarnate life as the Son of man. Because He is the same yesterday, today, and forever, we are not surprised to read that when He entered this world, the moral law was within His heart.[14] More than that, He was made under that law,[15] meaning that by volunteering to be God's servant, He came to fulfill it and to obey it.[16]

We can therefore deduce the nature of Jesus' earthly life from the nature of the Ten Commandments. They tell us what His life was like toward God and toward man. They tell us what He was like outwardly and inwardly.[17] Where Israel, God's national son, failed repeatedly, Jesus, God's only begotten Son, succeeded perfectly, continuously, and gloriously.[18] Nothing less than this astounding, perfect, and complete righteousness of Christ is imputed to those who are united to Him by faith.[19]

An Example of Jesus' Teaching

The law shows us not just how Jesus lived but also what He taught. His first sermon was on the moral law, and as we would expect, He did not simply repeat it, but amplified, enhanced, and extended it.[20]

He also internalized the requirements of the ceremonial law. Instead of *physical* purity permitting access to the tabernacle, Jesus said, "Blessed are the pure in heart, for they shall see God."[21]

Jesus picked up Deuteronomy's teaching on the tithe and applied it to the widow's mite and the Pharisees' hypocrisy.[22] The more we read the two Testaments together, the more we will discover that the New Testament in general and Jesus' words in particular are permeated with Old Testament vocabulary and concepts.

An Examination in Jesus' Light

The Westminster Confession of Faith says that the law helps believers discover "the sinful pollutions of their nature, hearts and lives; so as, examining themselves thereby, they may come to further conviction of, humiliation for, and hatred against sin; together with a clearer sight of the need they have of Christ, and the perfection of His obedience."[23]

The Israelites must often have experienced conviction of sin under the law and felt the fearful impact of its curses. But as a result, they must also have seen more clearly their need of deliverance. Their disobedience testified to the fact that they needed God to act in a new, redemptive way to write the law on their hearts.[24]

Thus, we should not be surprised that He whose character was exhibited in the law, He whose life expounded the law, and He who so perfectly taught the law should have, at times, the same convicting effects on people as the law did. When the devils and evil spirits saw Him, they cried out with fear and terror.[25] When Peter saw His holiness, he exclaimed, "Depart from me, for I am a sinful man, O Lord!"[26]

The moral law, as taught and exemplified by Jesus, prepares the way for the gospel of grace.[27] That was why John Paton began his mission to the pagans of the New Hebrides not with John 3:16 but with the Ten Commandments and why John Eliot's first sermon to the Native Americans was also the Ten Commandments.

An Explanation of Jesus' Death

The law not only reveals our need for Jesus' death but also explains the *nature* of it:

- *The transgression of the law.* The death of Jesus was the greatest act of lawlessness ever perpetrated. If His life demonstrated the law in an unprecedented way, His death showed lawlessness in a similarly unprecedented way.

- *The curses of the law.* The curses of the law were executed upon Jesus so that His people would be freed from the same curse.[28] Just as Jesus' obedience to the law's precepts came to a climax on the cross, so did His suffering of the law's penalties. If you want to better understand what Jesus suffered for His people, study the law's penalties and curses in Deuteronomy and Leviticus.

- *The justice of the law.* Vern Poythress identifies four essential principles of Old Testament justice that anticipate and foreshadow God's justice in the death of Jesus:

First, the principle of *retribution* is "eye for eye, tooth for tooth."[29] In Jesus' death we see the infliction of divine retribution on Him for the sins of those He represented—eye for eye, hand for hand, life for life, soul for soul: "Who Himself bore our sins *in His own body* on the tree."[30]

Second, we see *restitution*, the necessity of compensating those whose persons, property, and names we have harmed.[31] The New Testament picks up on this idea and presents Jesus' death as a ransom.[32] That was why Jesus was prophesied as saying, "Though I have stolen nothing, I still must restore it."[33]

Third, one of the great principles of Old Testament justice was *deterrence.* Justice was to be so enacted that observers would be deterred from the sins that required it.[34] The apostle Paul expounded the cross of Jesus as the ultimate sin deterrent.[35]

Fourth, Old Testament justice also provided for the *rehabilitation* of the offender under certain circumstances. This indicates that Jesus' death also had the ultimate aim of rehabilitating sinners, which is confirmed by many New Testament references.[36]

The Extent of Jesus' Death

Just as the law was concerned with reversing the effects of sin on the whole creation, so, in some significant ways, Jesus' death reversed the creation-wide effects of sin. Just as sin had cosmic dimensions, so, in some important regards, Jesus' death did too. Though not intended to save every sinner in the world, Jesus' death did have as one of its ultimate aims the restoration of order and life to a disordered and dying world.[37]

The Execution of Jesus' Judgment

The divine punishments in the Old Testament were not arbitrary but expressions of who God is. And because Jesus will execute the final divine penalties,[38] Old Testament penalties are also expressions of who Jesus is. The penalties attached to the law and their execution anticipate the final judgment that will fall on the disobedient and the ungodly. They are faint shadows or mini examples of Jesus' final judgment, and they are sent to compel sinners to seek safety in the Savior.

The Enjoyment of Jesus' Presence

The moral law shows us Jesus' power to curse disobedience and His power to bless obedience.[39] The keeping of the law did not and could not save, but it was linked to the flourishing and enjoyment of spiritual life in the saved soul. If redeemed Israel separated from sin, death, and uncleanness, they would enjoy more and more of God's blessed presence among them.[40] As we've already seen, that gracious order is so important to grasp: redemption, relationship, rules, and then reward.[41] Like Israel, we are *redeemed* by mercy, brought into a living *relationship* with Jesus, for which we show our gratitude by obeying His *rules*, which He in turn also graciously *rewards* with more of His presence.

Loving obedience brings Jesus into the soul and the soul to Jesus: "He who has My commandments and keeps them, it is he who loves Me. And he who loves Me will be loved by My Father, and I will love him and manifest Myself to him."[42] We express our love to Jesus by obedience to His unchanging moral law, and this loving law-keeping opens a channel through which Jesus communicates more of His love to us.

An Entrance into Jesus' Home

The order the law was intended to establish was never fully realized for Israel—neither in the wilderness nor in the promised land. The promised land was but an imperfect foreshadowing of the Lord's ideal home and dwelling place. And despite many subsequent attempts to create an earthly utopia, the dream continues to elude us. It is only in heaven that we will see the law's order perfectly and beautifully honored and practiced—holy worship, holy rest, holy relationships, holy conversation, and holy everything and everyone.

The law therefore gives us a description of Jesus' present holy habitation, the place in which He resides and from which He reigns—and the place where we hope to join Him one day.

THE EXALTATION OF JESUS' GLORY

The Westminster Confession of Faith says that the law gives believers "a clearer sight of the need they have of Christ, and the perfection of His obedience."[43] The law therefore exalts Jesus in the believer's mind and heart.

Even our imperfect obedience to the moral law exalts Jesus. We magnify Him by worshipping Him as God in the way He appointed. We lift Him up by treasuring His name, the name above every name. We honor Him by resting in Him and resting on His day. We revere Him when we honor the roles and relationships with which He has blessed us. We elevate Him when we value the life He has created. We applaud Him when we tell the truth and spread His truth. We exalt Him when we find Him more satisfying than any earthly possession.

Christopher Wright highlighted that the law had a missional purpose by shaping the nation in the image of God:

The law had the function of shaping Israel to be that representative people, making the character and requirements of God known to the nations. That is a missional function. . . . The purpose of the law was to make Israel visibly different, in such a way that would draw interest and comment, and essentially bear witness to the God they worshipped.[44]

So it is with us today. And the more we use the ten methods outlined above, the more Jesus will be magnified and honored in us and in the world.

Just as He magnified the law and made it honorable,[45] so the law magnifies Him and makes Him honorable. Let us therefore use the law as a friend, not as an enemy. Let us use it as God intended, to magnify and honor Jesus in our lives.

CHAPTER 11

CHRIST'S PAST

Discovering Jesus in Old Testament History

I'm not very good at perceiving optical illusions. I can look at the black-and-white picture of that elegant lady in the feather hat for hours and not once can I get it also to look like a haggard lady in a shawl. And do you remember the craze for pictures that were made up of thousands of little pictures? Apparently if you looked long enough or defocused your eyes enough, a big picture eventually appeared from the confusion. Well, I could look for hours and blur my sight until it hurt, yet still not see any big picture. And my annoyance only increased as everyone else got the big picture with such evident delight.

But that optical illusion illustrates one way of connecting the Old Testament with Jesus. The New Testament enables us to look at the thousands of seemingly disconnected parts of the Old Testament in such a way that at last we see a big picture of Jesus emerge from all of it. That's a wonderful experience, isn't it?

I remember when I started coming across writers and preachers who were able to show how the whole Old Testament connects with Jesus and climaxes in His appearing. How my mind and heart rejoiced! And it was no optical or theological illusion either. It was exciting truth, delightful reality. Author Donald Miller compared God's plan of redemption to a play:

> "As a playwright works into the earlier scenes of his play certain ideas which are only perplexing at the time they are introduced, but which are made clear as one looks back to them from the standpoint of the climax, God was working into the earlier acts of the drama of redemption elements which, when recapitulated in a higher key in Jesus, received a clarity which they did not have in their original setting." . . . [Greidanus continues:] Because God progressively works out his redemptive plan in human history, the New Testament writers can preach Christ from the Old Testament as the culmination of a long series of redemptive acts.[1]

Yes, that puts it so well. However, once I got over the initial rush of discovering the big picture, I began to notice that sometimes, in the desire to show that Jesus is the culmination or destination of Old Testament history, the little pictures of Jesus that make up the big picture were often being overlooked.

JESUS IN THE LITTLE PICTURES

Let me go back to the optical illusion to explain what I mean. Look closely at the little pictures again. What do you see? Usually it's just a bunch of unrelated and irrelevant items. For example, if the big picture is of George Washington, the little pictures may be images of carrots, bananas, horses, computers, books, and so forth. The small pictures on their own do not relate to or connect with George Washington. It's only when they are viewed as part of the big picture that they bring us to George Washington.

And unfortunately that's how some people view and use the Old Testament. They see Jesus emerge from the big picture at the end of Old Testament history—and that's good—but they do not see Him in all the little pictures that make up the big picture. They are only so many carrots, bananas, and so forth. For example, some see all the Old Testament priests as pointing forward to Jesus' priestly work, and they do that. Some see all the Old Testament kings as pointing forward to Jesus as King of all kings, and He is that. But is Jesus seen only at the end of these long lines of priests and kings? Does He emerge only from the picture when we look back with New Testament eyes? Sometimes that's the impression that's given. But where does that leave Old Testament believers? Did they simply put their trust in Aaron's priesthood and David's monarchy? No! By faith they saw the coming Messiah pictured in Aaron's priesthood and David's kingdom. They saw Jesus in the small pictures. True, they saw Him only in shadow form, but you don't see shadows without some light, do you?

Jonathan Edwards's *History of the Work of Redemption* really opened my eyes to seeing Jesus in the little pictures. The purpose of Edwards's book was to show the big picture of redemption, that God's work of redemption began not at Bethlehem but in the garden of Eden. He said that the work of redemption covered all that was done by the Father, the Spirit, and Christ as mediator before, during, and after His time in this world and went on to demon-strate how redemptive history unfolded throughout the Bible.[2]

Edwards also emphasized the redemption of individual souls along the way. He saw the "lesser salvations and deliverances for his church and people" as "images and forerunners of the great salvation Christ was to work out when he came."[3] Crucially he saw true Christian salvation in the "lesser salvations." And he showed how Jesus was not just the *end* of redemptive history but also an active participant throughout it. He was not just the last chapter for which all the others were setting the scene; He was present from the very first chapter and in every chapter of redemptive history.

Edwards did not underestimate the climactic nature of Jesus' incarnation. He did not deny that Jesus' person and work at His first coming were necessary to give redemptive significance to the Old Testament. He agreed that no Old Testament saint could ever have been saved without Jesus' coming to this earth. He did not, however, view the Old Testament events as only stepping-stones to Jesus. He saw Him in the stepping-stones themselves. He did not see the need to relate everything to the big picture; he could find the big picture even in the small pictures.

JESUS IN REDEMPTIVE HISTORY

There is no substitute for reading Edwards's *History of the Work of Redemption*. However, here I would like to highlight just a few extracts to give you samples of what is, I believe, the most Christ-honoring way of preaching Christ from His past, from Old Testament history:

THE FIRST SALVATION

Edwards found Christ as early as Genesis 3, in the first salvation of the Bible:

> As soon as man ever fell, Christ the eternal Son of God clothed himself with his mediatorial character and therein presented himself before the Father. He immediately stepped in between an holy, infinite, offended majesty and offending mankind, and was accepted in his interposition.... Christ began to exercise the office of mediator between God and man as soon as man fell because mercy began to be exercised towards man immediately.[4]

Edwards went on to show how Genesis 3:15–22 revealed Christ to Adam and Eve in His three offices of prophet (the promise of a seed to defeat the Devil), priest (the institution of sacrifices), and king (the salvation of Adam and Eve):

> Thus 'tis exceeding probable if not evident that as Christ took on him the work of a mediator as soon as (man fell) . . . he now immediately began his Work of Redemption in its effect. And that he immediately banished his great enemy, the devil whom he had undertaken to conquer, and rescued those two first captives.[5]

THE FIRST SACRIFICE

From the life of Abel, Edwards established that sacrifices were appointed by God to be a prophetic picture of the Messiah's sacrifice and that when offered through faith in the coming Messiah, they were pleasing to God. Also, from the fact that Abel seemed to be complying with an established custom, Edwards argued that sacrifice "was instituted immediately after God had revealed the covenant of grace in Gen. 3:15, which covenant and promise was the foundation on which the custom of sacrificing was built."[6]

THE FIRST GLORIFICATION

The first persecution was followed by the first martyrdom, when Cain slew righteous Abel. Edwards said that Abel's soul was

> the first that went to heaven through Christ's redemption. . . . If [Abel] was the first, then as the redemption of Christ began to dawn before in the souls of men in their conversion and justification, in him it first began to dawn in glorification. And in him the angels began first to do the part of ministering spirits to Christ in going forth to conduct the souls of the redeemed to glory. And in [Abel] the elect angels in heaven had the first opportunity to see so wonderful a sight as the soul of one of the fallen race of mankind, that had been sunk by the fall into such an abyss of sin and misery actually brought to heaven in the enjoyment of heavenly glory.[7]

THE FIRST REVIVAL

Edwards persuasively argued that the days of Enos, in which men began "to call upon the name of the LORD,"[8] were the "first remarkable pouring out of the Spirit of God that ever was. There had [been] a saving work of God in the hearts of some before, but now God was pleased to grant a more large effusion of his Spirit for the bringing in an harvest of souls to Christ."[9]

We must not think that the Holy Spirit began to be given at pentecost. At pentecost the Holy Spirit was given in greater measure and to a greater number. But as Old Testament believers were "dead in trespasses and sins," they could not begin to believe or repent without the Holy Spirit. And just like us, they could not continue one second in faith without the continuing work of the Holy Spirit.[10]

The Spirit's indwelling in the Old Testament was like a water dropper continually dripping a little water onto a sponge on a hot summer day. The sponge gets wet but never fills up so much that the water begins to run out of the sponge. The Spirit's indwelling in the New Testament era is more like a pressure washer jetting water into a sponge with excess water pouring out everywhere. When the fullness of God's revelation of Jesus had come, the fullness of the Spirit could be poured out.[11] At pentecost we see a new plenitude, perpetuity, pervasiveness, and publicity about the Holy Spirit. We see Him work more intensively, extensively, and obviously.

This difference in degree and depth must not lead us to deny the Holy Spirit's constant indwelling work in Old Testament believers. No one can be born again, believe, or repent without the inward work of the Holy Spirit. And no one can stay a believer for one second without the ongoing internal work of the Holy Spirit—neither in the Old nor in the New Testament. Without the Holy Spirit constantly in and at work in our hearts, believers would immediately apostatize.

THE FIRST PREACHER

Edwards viewed Enoch as a greater saint than any before him. He therefore experienced the work of redemption to a greater degree than any before him, being brought into intimate fellowship with Christ.[12] The New Testament reveals that Enoch was also a preacher of Christ.[13] Edwards noted,

Here Enoch prophesies of the coming of Christ. It doesn't seem to be confined to any particular coming of Christ, but it has respect in general to Christ's coming in his kingdom, and is fulfilled in a degree in both the first and second coming of Christ, and indeed in every remarkable manifestation Christ has made of himself in the world for the saving of his people and the destroying of his enemies.[14]

The First "Resurrection"

The uniqueness of God's work of redemption in Enoch is highlighted by his "translation" into heaven.[15] Edwards wrote, "Now this translation of Enoch was the first instance that ever was of restoring the ruins of the fall with respect to the body. There had been many instances of restoring the soul of man by Christ's redemption, but none of redeeming and actually saving the body till now."[16]

And so Edwards went on. These samples provide only a flavor of Edwards's *History of Redemption*. Again, I urge you to read it for yourself and enjoy the spiritual beauty and simplicity of his Christ-centered words. In sum, Edwards regarded Jesus and His redemption not only as the climax of redemptive history but also as an integral, constant part of all redemptive history. And that's no illusion!

Jesus' Use of Redemptive History

But there's yet another way of using Old Testament history in a Christ-centered way, and that's to consider how Jesus Himself was educated, motivated, and guided by the histories of the Old

Testament. I started thinking more deeply about this largely unexplored area when I was preparing a sermon on how Jesus learned, and it got me thinking about some implications of His humanness.[17]

Jesus' Humanity Needed Teaching

We are not here speaking of Jesus' divine mind, which was all-knowing. We are speaking of His finite and limited human mind. He was not born with perfect knowledge of everything. There were things He did not know—even divine things.[18]

Jesus Grew in Knowledge

As He aged and matured, He also developed in His knowledge and understanding.

Jesus Learned by Listening, Reading, and Studying

Although there were undoubtedly times when the Holy Spirit revealed truth directly to His human mind, He usually learned in the normal human way—by listening, reading, and so on.

Jesus' Most Important Source of Knowledge Was the Old Testament

The Old Testament was Jesus' most important book. His knowledge of it came to Him through His parents' teaching, His own reading, and His hearing it read and preached in the synagogue.

Jesus Knew the Old Testament Better than Anyone Ever Did

In His short time on this earth Jesus studied it more effectively and with more understanding than anyone before or since.

Christopher Wright thought deeply and wrote beautifully about this area of Jesus' life and introduced his own insights with this thought-provoking passage:

> In the midst of the many intrinsically fascinating reasons why Old Testament study is so rewarding, the most exciting to me is the way it never fails to add new depths to my understanding of Jesus. I find myself aware that in reading the Hebrew Scriptures I am handling something that gives me a closer common link with Jesus than any archaeological artifact could do. For these are the words he read. These were the stories he knew. These were the songs he sang. These were the depths of wisdom and revelation and prophecy that shaped his whole view of "life, the universe and everything." This is where he found his insights into the mind of his Father God. Above all, this is where he found the shape of his own identity and the goal of his own mission. In short, the deeper you go into understanding the Old Testament, the closer you come to the heart of Jesus. (After all, Jesus never actually read the New Testament!)[19]

Many mysteries remain in this area of what Jesus knew and how He learned. For example, what effect did the fact that He inspired the Old Testament have on His human knowledge? How much did Jesus learn directly, via the ministry of the Spirit? Did His human mind ever access His divine mind? However, the five points made above give us a sufficient basis to think about how much Jesus learned about Himself—His person and work—from various Old Testament passages. And as we do so, let's be careful to guard the typical ordinariness of His maturing humanity.

His Past

One of the most fundamental human questions is, where did I come from? It explains the deep interest of human beings in our ancestors. We want to know who led up to us. We value those who had a role in our past. We admire those whose wise or brave decisions contributed to what we are. We are humbled by the skeletons in our cupboards, by the discovery of the less virtuous characters and their roles in our own stories.

Jesus was no different. As the most important figure in all human history, He would have had a special interest in the history that led up to Him. With what fascination would He have listened to His parents' Bible stories? Would He not have had a special interest in, and love for, those whose wise and brave decisions contributed to His arrival and His identity? How He valued Israel, His "kinsmen according to the flesh."[20] But Gentiles also had a special place in His past; the only four mothers included in His genealogy were Gentiles.

And what about all the sinners in His family tree? They were not just ordinary sinners either: a pagan moon worshipper (Abraham), prostitutes (Tamar and Rahab), adulterers (David and Bathsheba), a child murderer and a persecutor (Manasseh), and so on. What lowly roots! What humble sympathy this family tree would give Him with lowly sinners!

His Person

When Jesus asked that very basic human question, "Who am I?" the Old Testament supplied a large part of the answer. Wright stated,

It was the Old Testament which helped Jesus to understand Jesus. Who did he think he was? What did he think he was to do? The answers came from his Bible, the Hebrew Scriptures in which he found a rich tapestry of figures, historical persons, prophetic pictures and symbols of worship. And in this tapestry, where others saw only a fragmented collection of various figures and hopes, Jesus saw his own face. His Hebrew Bible provided the shape of his own identity.[21]

When Jesus was asked, "Are You the Coming One, or do we look for another?" He pointed His questioners to the Old Testament where He had read detailed descriptions of His person.[22] How thrilled He must have been as He saw that He was the seed of Abraham through whom all the nations of the world would be blessed. How awed He must have been as a young child to gradually learn that He was the son of David whose kingdom and name would endure forever. How did He feel and respond when He read His numerous and varied Old Testament names: Messiah, Commander of the Lord's army, Counselor and Prince of Peace, Servant, Man of Sorrows, Rock, Lamb, and more?[23]

Above all, imagine what He learned about Himself from the nation of Israel. The New Testament presents Jesus as the perfect fulfillment and embodiment of all that Israel was meant to be and yet failed to be. Israel was put in the world as a uniquely privileged nation in order to reveal God and His redemption to the world.[24] And although Israel so dismally failed at this, Jesus dramatically succeeded. God completed through Jesus what had been left undone by Israel.

His Purpose

Having answered, where did I come from? and, who am I? the next major life question is, what am I here for? And the Old Testament again provided the primary source of Jesus' answer to this question. It provided Him with the models, pictures, and patterns that taught Him what He was here to do.

For example, think how much Jesus would have learned as He read about the Old Testament sacrifices. With what anxiety and apprehension He would have read about the transferring of guilt, the flaying, the bleeding, and the burning. However much greatness He saw in the temple, He knew one greater than the temple was here.[25] How He must have wept when He read in Isaiah of the hardness He predicted would characterize Israel's reaction to His sermons.[26] How much Jeremiah's tearful experience revealed to Him the painful response to be expected in Jerusalem as He labored night and day against the power of the religious establishment to save Jerusalem from certain destruction—only to be mocked and then branded a traitor. How much He learned of His suffering, entombment, and resurrection as He studied Jonah.[27] What hope of Gentile converts did the Queen of Sheba's visit to Solomon give to Him?[28] With what confidence He looked forward to the day of coronation when He read of David's enthronement.[29]

His Principles

The moral and spiritual principles of the Old Testament are prominent in Jesus' life and teaching. Throughout His whole life, He turned to these Scriptures to give Him clear guidance and direction, especially in resisting temptation.[30]

The Old Testament also influenced and informed the form and content of His teaching. His first major sermon was on the Mount, and His first point was the Beatitudes. Although many think that these "blessings" are something new, both form and content are from the Old Testament.[31] Pastor and lecturer Richard T. France said, "The Sermon on the Mount, though it contains few formal quotations from the Old Testament, is so permeated with both Old Testament words and ideas that hardly any part of its teaching is not to some degree modeled on, or at least paralleled in, the Old Testament."[32]

His People

As we have seen, Jesus learned much about Himself from His study of what Israel was meant to be. But He also learned much about His people, His New Testament people, from the descriptions of Old Testament Israel. France said that there is plenty of evidence to suggest that Jesus viewed His disciples as "the continuing people of God, the true Israel, in whom the hopes and the destiny of Old Testament Israel were to find fulfillment."[33] However, like the apostle Paul, I do not believe the cutting off of the natural branches (Israel) or the incorporation of the wild branches (the Gentiles) preclude a later regrafting of the natural branches, to the even greater blessing of the church of Christ.[34]

His Praises

We can also tell a lot about a person from his choice of music, the songs he likes to sing. The Old Testament psalms were Jesus' songs; they comprised His hymnbook. Wright noted that "Jesus came to a people who knew how to pray, and to sing. The rich heritage of worship in Israel was part of the very fabric and furniture of the mind of Jesus. So it is not at all surprising to find him often quoting from the Psalms, even with his dying breath."[35]

In His human nature Jesus worshipped God perfectly. In doing so, He used the perfect materials of praise—the Psalms. We'll explore this subject further in a later chapter, "Christ's Poets," but next time you read the Psalms, why not think about how Jesus read them and sang them?

THE TRUE GOD-MAN

Because much mystery surrounds this area of how Jesus learned in His humanity, we should be suggestive rather than dogmatic when exploring these themes. But we also must retain the full humanity of Jesus. Pastor John MacArthur commented on Luke 2:52:

> Luke is saying that every aspect of Jesus' development into full manhood (intellectually, spiritually, and socially) was ordinary not extraordinary. . . . His conscious mind was therefore subject to the normal limitations of human finitude. In other words, as Luke says here, Jesus truly *learned* things. Although He knew everything exhaustively and omnisciently as God, He did not always maintain full awareness of everything in His human consciousness. The questions He asked those rabbis were part of the learning process, not some backhanded way of showing the rabbis up. He was truly learning from them and processing what they taught Him.[36]

In his unique article on the human development of Jesus, Princeton professor B. B. Warfield talked about the sincerity of Jesus' questions: "He repeatedly is represented as seeking knowledge through questions, which undoubtedly were not asked only to give the appearance of a dependence on information from without that was not real with him: he is made to express surprise; and to make trial of new circumstances."[37] Warfield warned that we commit errors when we grasp and emphasize one nature but openly discard the other. Worship along with him in this rich paragraph:

> The glory of the incarnation is that it presents to our adoring gaze not a humanized God or a deified man, but a true God-man—one who is all that God is and at the same time all that man is: on whose almighty arm we can rest, and to whose human sympathy we can appeal. We cannot afford to lose either the God in the man or the man in the God; our hearts cry out for the complete God-man whom the Scriptures offer us.[38]

CHAPTER 12

CHRIST'S PROPHETS

*Discovering Jesus in the Old
Testament Prophets*

A part from some well-known verses that clearly predict Jesus, the Old Testament prophets remain largely unchartered territory for most of us. We open Jeremiah and wonder, is it worth the effort? Perhaps we then try a "minor" prophet like Joel and wonder what locust plagues have to do with the digital revolution. The country, culture, and chronology gaps are huge and seem to be unbridgeable. But are they? Are these numerous books completely irrelevant to the twenty-first-century Christian? Not if they reveal Jesus. And they do. And they do so in many varied and remarkable ways.

Certainly a bit of work is required to find the seams of gold in these messianic mines, but I hope to persuade you that the rewards are worth the extra effort, and I want to do some of the heavy lifting for you. But before we look at the prophets'

Christ-centered message, let's pause a moment to consider the Christ-centered nature of the prophets' office.

THE MINISTRY OF THE PROPHETS

The secret to understanding the prophets is first of all to travel back a thousand years or so to Moses and the book of Deuteronomy. There, Moses told us that the office of the Old Testament prophet was designed, instituted, and developed by God to prepare His people for Jesus Christ, His ultimate and final Prophet.[1] Therefore, when we read the Old Testament prophets, we should look for the aspects or features of their office or ministry that predict the prophetic office of Jesus Christ. Here are some to watch for:

OUR NEED

First, consider the *reason* for prophets. They were needed to stand between God and sinners and to speak God's word in God's place. God installed Moses as His first official prophet to Israel because the Israelites were too terrified to hear God speak directly to them.[2] But even Moses knew He was not God's last word to His people; he predicted an even greater prophet who would come after him.[3] And despite God's raising up and sending great prophets throughout the Old Testament, the Israelites realized that the greatest prophet had still not come. That's why when Jesus burst on the scene, many rightly wondered whether He was the ultimate promised prophet of God.[4]

Every Old Testament prophet reminds us of our need for a prophetic mediator and anticipates God's provision of Jesus Christ, the Prophet.

Divine Calling

Second, remember who *raised* up the prophets. God took the initiative and called Moses into the prophetic office. This emphasis on the divine initiative, call, and authorization is evident in the lives of many Old Testament prophets.[5]

The divine calling and commissioning of every Old Testament prophet point toward the divine calling and commissioning of Jesus Christ, the Prophet.

Varied Descriptions

Third, the varied *representations* of the prophets revealed the varied dimensions of their ministries. For example, the Hebrew word for prophet means "a called person." Its Greek translation can mean "to tell forth (preach) or foretell (predict)." Other designations include a seer (of visions), a servant, a messenger, a watchman, or simply the man of God.

Every designation or description of a prophet reveals a little about the one Prophet who fitted these designations perfectly, Jesus Christ.

Divine Revelations

Fourth, the prophet received divine *revelations*. The prophet's message was the result not of his own reasoning, insight, or observations but of divine revelation. God said, "[I] will put My words in His mouth . . . He shall speak to them all that I command Him."[6] The prophet had a strict concern to communicate the exact words spoken to him—the truth, the whole truth, and nothing but the truth.

The carefulness and faithfulness with which the prophets heard and spoke the exact words of God, no more and no less, build expectation of the supreme carefulness and faithfulness with which Jesus Christ, the Prophet, heard and spoke what God revealed to Him.[7]

COVENANTAL ROLES

Fifth, the prophet had a covenantal *role*. Powerful ancient Near Eastern kings, sometimes called suzerains, often made covenants with weaker kings (vassals), in which they promised the vassals certain benefits if they proved loyal, and they threatened punishment if the vassals did not. The suzerains then sent emissaries to promise blessings for obedience and to prosecute violations.

The use of similar emissarial language in the prophets' speeches deepens our understanding of the prophet's role. Jehovah was the great Suzerain who sent prophets as His mediators and emissaries to ensure covenant faithfulness in His vassal, Israel, to prosecute covenant violations, and to ensure the safety and prosperity of the faithful.

When the prophets mediate God's covenant, they point forward to Jesus Christ, the ultimate Messenger of God's covenant.

REJECTION

Sixth, all the prophets faced opposition and *rejection*. Starting with the first false prophet's "Has God said?" in the garden of Eden, all of God's prophets have been contradicted in the ongoing spiritual battle with the father of lies and his mouthpieces.

The rejection of God's messengers and their messages prefigured the rejection of God's greatest Messenger and Message, Jesus Christ.

THE PERFECT PROPHET

Seventh, let me underline that the prophetic office was ultimately *realized* in Christ. As with all Old Testament institutions and offices, there was a divinely in-built inadequacy in the office of the Old Testament prophet and in all who tried to fill that office.

Every deficiency or inadequacy in the Old Testament prophets contrasts with the fullness and perfection of Jesus Christ, the Prophet of God. We see that looking back, but the Old Testament believers also saw that looking forward.

Having briefly considered the ministry of the prophets and how even that office pointed forward to the ultimate Office Bearer, let's now examine what the prophets actually said.

The Message of the Prophets

The first time an apprentice engineer looks at a locomotive engine, he has little idea where to start. That's why apprentice engineers are issued with numerous step-by-step guides. When we open the "engine" of the prophets, we often feel like that apprentice, don't we? Where do I start? What do I do now? I still feel like that from time to time, but I've gradually found that these three steps help me to process and understand their message.

Step 1: The Original Message (The Engine)

If a train engineer skips over the first chapter of the manual, danger and damage are around the corner. Similar damage results if we skip over the vital first step of asking, what did this prophet's message mean to the original readers? Yet in the rush to apply the Bible to our lives, that's what many of us do. Two questions in particular, if answered correctly, will keep us on the right track.

What are the historical circumstances? An engineer wants to know a bit of background before he pulls out a wrench: model, year, mileage, past problems, recent events, and so on. Without this information, he's going to jump to the wrong conclusions. Similarly we must pause and spend time to figure out the historical and geographical background of the prophets' messages. So many mistakes are made by jumping straight from 700 BC to AD 2000. We must ask how the original hearers understood the prophets' message and how they applied that to their own lives and circumstances.

What kind of writing is this? The majority of the prophetic writings explain Israel's past and present experience rather than the future. The prophets demonstrate to Israel that previous divine prophecies of blessing for obedience and punishment for disobedience are being fulfilled to the letter. Such past and present messages still have a futuristic dimension insofar that they demonstrate how the principles of God's government are reliably constant and therefore predict how God will continue to deal with His people in all ages.[8]

At other times, the prophets do look beyond the past and the present to predict the future. Sometimes they do so in very clear, literal, straightforward terms. At other times they communicate in poetry or song, and sometimes they use highly symbolic words, often called apocalyptic language.[9]

It is absolutely vital to distinguish between these different kinds of writing. For example, a biography about a war president, such as Franklin D. Roosevelt, conveys its message in a different way than a based-on-a-true-story novel about a Second World War soldier fighting his way through France. British wartime singer Vera Lynn's moving wartime songs also connect us with the painful losses and soaring victories of war. All three media communicate the same message but do so in different ways. Similarly we must recognize that our approach to understanding the prophets will vary according to the kind of writing they use.

EXAMPLES: In Micah 5:2, the prophet predicts that Bethlehem will be the birthplace of the Messiah. The language and context are literal rather than symbolic and lead to the expectation of a literal birth in literal Bethlehem. In Ezekiel 47:1, the prophet predicts that floods of waters will flow out of the door of a massive future temple in Jerusalem. However, this takes place in a vision full of symbolic language, so we should interpret the prophecy in a symbolic way. The New Testament confirms this when Jesus said His body is the new temple and that His Spirit fulfills the flood of refreshing water.[10]

STEP 2: THE FULFILLMENT(S) (THE TRACK)

Once the engineer has started the engine, he must choose a set of tracks to test his work. There are numerous tracks to choose from, each of which will take him to a different destination, so he must choose the right one for that particular train. Likewise, when we want to move forward with the prophets to see how their messages were fulfilled down the line, we must choose the right track if we are to arrive at the right destination. Here are a few possibilities:

Explicit fulfillment. Many fulfillments are relatively easy to identify because they are often preceded in the New Testament by an introductory formula such as, "That it might be fulfilled . . ." There is a specific detailed prediction matched with a specific detailed fulfillment.

EXAMPLE: In Zechariah 9:9, the prophet predicts that Israel's king will come riding on, of all things, a donkey. This prophecy was fulfilled to the letter in Matthew 21:4–5. Such prediction-fulfillment is saying something much more than that Jesus was the somewhat unexpected climax of the Old Testament. Rather, it is rightfully claiming that Old Testament prophets expected Jesus, described Him in considerable detail, and would not have been surprised at the way He fulfilled their predictions.

Implicit fulfillment. In other prophecies, the predictive element is plain, but the New Testament fulfillment makes no explicit connection with it. Perhaps the link is too obvious to merit a mention, or maybe the New Testament writer relied on the reader's knowledge of the Old Testament to make the link for himself.

EXAMPLE: Balaam prophesied that a star and a scepter would be associated with the Messiah.[11] When a star led the wise men to the infant King, Matthew did not explicitly refer to the fulfillment.[12] The implied fulfillment, however, was made explicit later in the Bible.[13] Walter Kaiser highlighted how the book of Revelation "probably contains more OT imagery and phrases than any other NT writing, yet it does not contain a single formal quotation from the OT."[14]

"Hindsight" fulfillment. In some cases the prophetic content of the original Old Testament words becomes clear only in the light of New Testament revelation. It's only when the fulfillment takes place that the prophetic nature of the original passage becomes clear.

EXAMPLE: Matthew 13:35 tells us that Jesus' teaching of the crowd in parables was a fulfillment of Psalm 78:2, which does not appear to be predictive at all in its original context. Sidney Greidanus explains, "Matthew looks back at the Old Testament from the reality of Christ. . . . 'Matthew sees the whole Old Testament as the embodiment of promise. . . . Hence all kinds of OT writing (not just prophecies) can be drawn on in relating that promise to Jesus.'"[15]

Theological fulfillment. This describes the way that theological themes from the Old Testament are not only carried over into the New Testament but also raised, heightened, widened, deepened, and so fulfilled.

EXAMPLE: The servant theology of John's gospel and Philippians 2 is a fulfillment of the well-known Old Testament servant motif.[16]

Combined fulfillment. Sometimes the New Testament writers cite more than one Old Testament passage as being fulfilled at one time.

EXAMPLE: "[Jesus] said to them, 'It is written, "My house shall be called a house of prayer," but you have made it a "den of thieves."'"[17]

Summary fulfillment. Four times the New Testament citation of the Old Testament cannot be traced to a specific Old Testament source.[18] Walter Kaiser and other Old Testament scholars have called these "quotations of substance" or "concise summaries of the teaching of various parts of the older Scriptures."[19] These fulfillments point back not to one passage or even one prophet in particular but to the canon of Old Testament scripture in general.

EXAMPLE: The Old Testament as a whole predicted that the Messiah would have to pass through obscurity and humiliation before being glorified.[20] That helps us understand why Matthew cited Jesus' being a Nazarene as a fulfillment of Old Testament prophecy.[21] Nazareth is not mentioned in the Old Testament, never mind as the predicted home of the Messiah. However, as the most obscure and insignificant village in Israel, it was a fitting place for the Messiah to begin fulfilling this prophetic theme from the Old Testament.

Single fulfillment. Some fulfillments are singular in nature; they are fulfilled in one particular event. These are relatively easy to identify and expound.

EXAMPLE: Micah 5:2 predicted the birthplace of the Messiah as Bethlehem, and Matthew noted the single fulfillment of this prophecy.[22]

Multiple fulfillments. There can also be multiple fulfillments of a single prophecy. An example would be the prophetic predictions of salvation for the Gentiles.[23] This was not fulfilled in a single event but has been fulfilled repeatedly, especially since the first coming of Christ.

Many predictions made by Old Testament prophets, also by Jesus and His apostles, *commenced* fulfillment in events associated with the first coming of Jesus; they *continue* to be fulfilled in events associated with church history from the New Testament age right up to the present; and they will have *consummate* or climactic fulfillment in events associated with the second coming of Jesus. So, the Bible's predictions are often fulfilled in phases—in three phases to be precise. There are filling, further filling, and then a filling full—a final fulfillment.

EXAMPLE: Ezekiel predicted a rebuilt temple after the Exile and the restoration. However, the temple he predicted was far too big for Mount Zion and spilled over into the surrounding countryside.[24] These promises really begin to be fulfilled on a larger and on a spiritual scale with the first coming of Jesus Christ, who instituted the New Testament church. They continue to be fulfilled as the church grows throughout the world, and they will achieve consummate fulfillment when the heavenly Jerusalem will be populated with an innumerable company of saints of every tribe, nation, and so on.

Staged fulfillment. Multiple fulfillments are the result of one prophetic seed growing, expanding, and developing over the years. Staged fulfillment is the result of the one prediction containing two prophetic seeds, one of which flowers at one stage in history and the other at another, later stage in history. From the distant perspective of the original prophet, it often looks like one seed and flower. But with the passage of time, it becomes clear that his prophecy joined events belonging to different times into one, making them seem like one single event.

EXAMPLE: In Isaiah 61, Isaiah predicted a time of great blessing and of great judgment.[25] When Jesus read this prophecy in the synagogue, He stopped His reading short of the promise of vengeance, intimating that the fulfillment of this prophecy would be in two stages: the first stage of blessing would be associated with His first coming and the second stage of judgment at His second coming.[26]

Essential fulfillment. Sometimes the prophets predict the future using the concepts and language of past events. However, they are not predicting an exact repetition. They are saying that the essential elements of past events will be seen again, usually in an even greater way.

EXAMPLE: The exodus was not only the most important redemptive event in the Old Testament; it also provided the redemptive language and concepts for a large number of prophetic predictions.[27] This led Israel to expect something similar to the exodus redemption, though higher and better, in the future.

Symbolic fulfillment. In contrast to specific prophecies, many are framed using symbolic language. Some think that if prophecy predicts historical events, and it does, then it must be written like history. There are occasions when the New Testament matches literal historic fulfillments with literal historic predictions. However, in many cases, it does not.[28] Christopher Wright says that the use of symbolism in prophecy explains why the material fulfillment of the promise may be different from the literal form of the original promise and yet still be a valid fulfillment of it. He turns to horses and cars to illustrate.

> Imagine a father who, in the days before mechanized transport, promises his son, aged 5, that when he is 21 he will give him a horse for himself. Meanwhile the motorcar is invented. So, on his 21st birthday the son awakes to find a motorcar outside, "with love from Dad." It would be a strange son who would accuse his father of breaking his promise just because there was no horse. And even stranger if, in spite of having received the far superior motorcar, the son insisted that the promise would only be fulfilled if a horse *also* materialized, since that was the literal promise. It is obvious that with the change in circumstances, unknown at the time the promise was made, the father has more than kept his promise. In fact he has done so in a way that *surpasses* the original words of the promise, which were necessarily limited by the mode of transport available at that time. The promise was made in terms understood at the time. It was fulfilled in the light of new historical events.[29]

EXAMPLE: When Joel predicted the greater spiritual blessings of the new covenant, he did so by speaking of a more general and common seeing of visions and dreams.[30] He did that because in Joel's day great spiritual blessing was usually associated with visions and dreams of divine things. However, when this prophecy was fulfilled, the previous medium of God's communicating—through symbolic dreams and visions—had been superseded by much clearer and more direct speech. That was why on the day of Pentecost and throughout the New Testament, we do not find lots of dreams and visions, but we do find a widespread and unprecedented outpouring of inspired truth through the apostles. Wright says, "To look for direct fulfillments of, say, Ezekiel in the 20th-century Middle East is to bypass and short-circuit the reality and the finality of what we already have in Christ as the fulfillment of those great assurances. It is like taking delivery of the motorcar but still expecting to receive a horse."[31]

Before we move on to the present message of the prophets, it's worth noting how confidently and persuasively the apostles appealed to New Testament fulfillment of Old Testament prophecies. Throughout the book of Acts, their basic appeal to the most skeptical of Jewish and Gentile hearers was simple and consistent: Jesus is both Lord and Christ, the exact and perfect fulfillment of Old Testament prophecies.[32]

STEP 3: THE PRESENT MESSAGE (THE DESTINATION)

We started off by finding out the original message to the original audience. We've taken various prophecies along different tracks of fulfillment and, I hope, arrived at the right destination to stop (or pause). The carriage doors have opened, and the guard is calling out to the passengers on the platform. He has a message to the heathen nations and a message to the church of Christ. Let's look at these in turn.

MESSAGE TO THE HEATHEN NATIONS

With the exceptions of Hosea and Haggai, all the prophetic books contain messages to the heathen nations that were oppressing God's people.[33] The prophets had two kinds of messages for these nations: judgment and salvation.

Judgment on the nations. Israel's enemies were national fulfillments of God's promise of hostility between His Seed and the Devil's.[34] But the Bible also uses these nations as typical examples of the future opposition that will be faced by God's New Testament people.

For example, Jesus said that the future Antichrist would be like Antiochus Epiphanes, who persecuted Israel between the Testaments, as Daniel predicted.[35] Revelation predicts that the ever-present enemies of God's people will be like Babylon, Egypt, Sodom, Gog, and Magog.[36] So, when we read the prophets' judgments on these heathen peoples and nations, we are also reading of God's certain judgment on all the enemies of God's people throughout history and ultimately and completely at the end of time.[37]

But we can go even deeper. Just as these nations' murderous enmity toward Israel demonstrated the Devil's intention to wipe out the Messiah by wiping out the nation that would father Him, these nations also illustrate and give visible form to the invisible principalities and powers that were ranged against Jesus when He lived in this world. Therefore, the prophetic messages of doom on the heathen nations prefigure the doom that Jesus heaped upon the spiritual powers behind these persecuting nations when He died and rose again.[38] These Old Testament words of doom on the enemies of God and His people are therefore full of comfort for God's people today. And they are also warnings to present-day nations and peoples about how God deals with those who defy Him and persecute His people.

Salvation for the nations. Although the prophets' messages contained much that was negative for the nations, there was also, at times, a redemptive purpose in their oracles. Jonah's ministry to the Ninevites demonstrated that God's messages of judgment were given to warn and provide opportunity to repent and turn to God. Prophetic predictions, then, were partly designed to motivate the hearers to trust and obey the Lord in order to escape His judgments and receive His blessings. But there is more than the implicit possibility of redemption in these messages. Specific nations are also encouraged, from time to time, with promises of a share in Israel's redemption, despite their mistreatment of Israel.[39] On top of that, there are the general promises of Gentile salvation, which pepper the prophets' writings.[40] What bright glimmers of hope this gave to even the most vicious of God's enemies, then and now.

Increasingly heavy Old Testament hints of Gentile inclusion in God's redemptive purposes find their fulfillment in Christ's ministry. Apart from the call to repentance and faith implicit in Jesus' warnings to the nations, He also predicted that the gospel would be preached to all nations, and then He commanded this to be so.[41] He began His earthly ministry in "Galilee of the Gentiles" and promised that they would share in the salvation offered to Israel.[42] His last words were full of hope to people in heathen darkness.[43]

MESSAGE TO THE CHURCH

The majority of the prophets' writings were addressed to Israel. Although the prophets usually begin their messages with strong notes of condemnation and judgment for unfaithful Israel, most of them end on a note of promise and hope for the repentant remnant. Is that therefore the key to applying the prophets' messages to Israel today? We take the hope-filled passages and offer them to the repentant remnant in the church of our own day?

Yes and no.

Yes, in the sense that the New Testament presents the church as the fulfillment of Israel. Although the apostle Paul gave us grounds to hope that many of ethnic Israel will yet turn to the Lord in the future,[44] the New Testament presents the New Testament church as the continuation of Israel, the Old Testament church.[45]

No, in the sense that the New Testament presents Jesus as the primary and ultimate fulfillment of Israel. We are going to look at four ways in which Jesus fulfilled Israel's history. But first let's look at how the present-day church should hear the messages that God originally gave to Israel.

ISRAEL AND THE CHURCH

God speaks an unchanging Word. The majority of the prophets' time was spent not predicting the future but pointing Israel to its past, to God's Word to them, and to God's works among them. Although Israel had many human voices contradicting God's voice and offering more palatable messages, the prophets never compromised. They kept expounding and applying God's Word, especially the gracious promises and fearful threats of Deuteronomy. Like Israel, the church and the individual believer need not new revelation but renewed faithfulness to God's existing revelation. Instead of listening to modern human voices, we need to open our ears to God's ancient voice.

God requires faith and repentance. Being an Israelite brought many national, economic, social, and spiritual privileges and blessings. But being an Israelite did not guarantee salvation. Outward privileges and outward observance saved no one. God wanted more than circumcised foreskins; He wanted circumcised hearts. God wanted more than bleeding and burning sacrifices; He wanted the broken spirit and contrite heart that showed they understood what their sins deserved. God wanted more than temple attendance; He wanted to dwell in the souls of His people. He wanted more than torn robes; He wanted torn hearts. He wanted more than washed bodies; He wanted clean hearts. Just like today's preachers, the prophets stressed again and again the need to move beyond the outward to the inward, beyond the externals to the internals, beyond the flesh to the spirit.

God chastises His people. God chose Israel to be a special people and nation and blessed Israel with His saving Word and works. However, these privileges did not secure Israel from divine discipline if they rejected His Word and despised His works. Indeed, the very fact that He loved them guaranteed corrective measures if they strayed from Him.[46] Israel's history gives the modern church and the individual believer such a vivid example of how this plays out. If you are in any doubt that the Lord chastens those whom He loves, just read the Old Testament prophets.

God preserves and comforts a remnant. Although it seems that the vast majority of Israel's people were blatant rebels, deceitful hypocrites, or apathetic worldlings, there were always a small number of true believers among them whom the prophets sought to comfort with promises and encouragements. Sometimes the prophets' messages were so full of doom and gloom for sinners, but then a beautiful burst of sunlight pierced and dispersed the darkness as the prophet turned to the believing remnant with heavenly comfort. Similarly today, the believing remnant in a church or nation sometimes suffers God's chastisement along with the rebels. However unlike the rebels, they may be given God's promises to support and strengthen them through the difficulties. Many suffering believers through the centuries have found incredible solace and help in the precious words of chapters like Isaiah 54 and Ezekiel 9.

God will send salvation. Almost every prophet moves from threat to promise. The book of Isaiah has thirty-nine chapters weighted heavily with threat but concludes with twenty-seven chapters heavy with glorious promises of salvation. The book of Amos has eight chapters of threat, but toward the end of the ninth and last chapter he, too, turns to beautiful promises of restoration. That's the general pattern of the prophets, and it's a hope-filled pattern. Together with that generally optimistic rhythm, there are multiple specific promises of the coming Messiah and His kingdom. Promise always has the last word.

ISRAEL AND JESUS

I mentioned previously that although the prophets' messages to Israel are often fulfilled in the church, they are ultimately fulfilled in Jesus. Let's now look at four ways in which He fulfilled Israel's history:

1. *Jesus' exodus.* The New Testament confirmed the prophets' expectations of Israel's history being repeated, though in a far higher sense, by presenting the Messiah as the One who repeated, recapitulated, epitomized, summed up, and so fulfilled Israel's history. For example, Jesus' flight to and return from Egypt is seen as a fulfillment of Israel's flight to and exodus from Egypt.[47] Hosea used Old Testa-

ment history to highlight God's goodness to His national "Son" Israel, in protecting and providing for Him through an Egyptian sojourn, supervised by a divinely sent Joseph. By the inspiration of the Holy Spirit, Matthew saw this as a prophetic paradigm, which predicted God's goodness to His only begotten "Son" Israel, in protecting and providing for Him through an Egyptian sojourn, supervised by a divinely sent Joseph. This, the early history of Israel, was reenacted in Jesus and ended with Him restored to God's land to fulfill God's task for Him. He is the Servant of the Lord in a way that Israel never was.

2. *Jesus' exile.* The exile and restoration of Israel and its Davidic king are the main focus of the prophetic books. The prophets had the task of preparing Israel for the devastation of its just exile, and of cultivating and maintaining hope for a future gracious divine restoration of the land and its Davidic king, a restoration that also would bless the world. Just as Israel's exodus prefigured the work of Jesus in redeeming Israel from its sins, so Israel's exile and restoration prefigured Jesus' exile for the sins of God's people and His subsequent glorious restoration, with a worldwide expansion of His kingdom.[48]

3. *Jesus' kingdom.* Despite great hopes for the Davidic monarchy, David and his successors failed to realize the ideal. Increasingly, whichever king Israel was given, it evoked the thought, *There must be someone better than this!* As this expectation and desire grew with each disappointment, so did the sense that no mere human being could fulfill these expectations. Thus, although the prophets never ceased to call the kings and the people to repentance,

they increasingly focused on the coming of an ideal king, a king larger than life, a king and a kingdom not of this world. Thus one of Jesus' first sermons was, "Repent, for the kingdom of heaven is at hand."[49] Jesus was saying, "The King has come, and He is setting up a kingdom."

4. *Jesus' day.* The prophets portray the Day of the Lord as a day of divine presence that would bring about judgment on God's enemies and deliverance of God's people. Some prophets described the "day of the LORD" as "near" or "at hand."[50] These imminent divine interventions, bringing divine judgment and deliverance, were predictive of a future and final Day of the Lord, a day in which the Lord would be present to save His people and judge His enemies.[51]

The New Testament takes up the language and concepts of Joel and other prophets to further develop the Bible's teaching about the Day of the Lord as a day of military devastation and judgment on sinners before righteousness can reign among God's delivered people.[52] In Jesus' first coming we can see the dawn of the Day of the Lord. But the high noon of the Day of the Lord is the day of Jesus' second and final coming. That day of unprecedented divine presence will be a day of final judgment for the unrepentant and a day of full inheritance for His people.

WE'VE FOUND HIM!

Whatever else the prophets were about, they were about Jesus. Paul said that his own preaching was exactly what the prophets preached: "Therefore, having obtained help from God, to this day

I stand, witnessing both to small and great, saying no other things than those which the prophets and Moses said would come—that the Christ would suffer, that He would be the first to rise from the dead, and would proclaim light to the Jewish people and to the Gentiles."[53]

May every reader of these words be able to say with Philip: "We have found Him of whom Moses in the law, and also the prophets, wrote—Jesus of Nazareth, the son of Joseph."[54]

CHAPTER 13

CHRIST'S PICTURES

*Discovering Jesus in the Old
Testament Types*

A picture is worth a thousand words. Pictures help us remember, understand, and look forward. When we want to *remember* our wedding, we don't get out our diaries or journals; we open the photo album. When we want to *understand* how a rocket works, we don't get out NASA's instruction manual; we look for some pictures. When we are *looking forward* to a vacation, we don't look up Wikipedia; we look up Google images. That's why God used so many pictures in the Old Testament. Vivid visuals like the Passover lamb, the Flood, or the tabernacle helped Israel *remember* better, *understand* better, and *look forward* better.

The study of how God used pictures to teach His people is usually called *typology*, not a terribly familiar word for most of us. Basically it means "picture-ology." It's a kind of visual theology. God pictured the truth to preach the truth.

Most of us run into two obstacles when we start thinking about typology. First, we don't do pictures. We are quite good at words and numbers: reading, science, technology, logic, and arithmetic. We like precision, clarity, and brevity. But we don't really do pictures: art, symbol, metaphor, meditation, poetry, and so on are strange to most of us. Propositional theology = good; visual theology = bad. This bias is a huge disadvantage when interpreting the Old Testament, which contains so many symbols and metaphors. Why didn't God just write an instruction manual?

The second obstacle is perhaps even more off-putting, and that's the way that typology has been so abused in the church. Most typology sermons resemble weird abstract art rather than something painted by Leonardo da Vinci. Whatever the preacher starts with in the Old Testament, he somehow gets to Jesus through various unpredictable leaps of logic and irrationality. Some hearers are stunned with the wonder of it all. Most look at the canvas and wonder what it's all about.

Since I discovered Jesus throughout the Old Testament, one of my passions has been to restore a sane, yet spiritually edifying typology to the church to help Christians profit not just from Jesus' prophetic words (as we saw in the last chapter) but from His prophetic pictures (typology). One problem is that there are few good modern books on the subject. People have been put off by so many bad examples of preaching from the types that they want nothing whatsoever to do with it.

The classic book *Typology of Scripture* by Scottish minister and theologian Patrick Fairbairn, who was an eminent nineteenth-century Scottish scholar, is a fine example of sound biblical scholarship. But like most books of that pre-cut-and-paste era, it is incredibly wordy, weighing in at seven hundred pages. What I'd like to do in this chapter is reduce those seven hundred pages to about ten. Let's start with the definition of a *type*:

A type is a real person, place, object, or event that God ordained to act as a predictive pattern or resemblance of Jesus' person and work, or of opposition to both. Let me unpack that a little:

- *A type is a real person, place, object, or event*: it is true, real, and factual—not a made-up allegory.
- *That God ordained*: it resembled Jesus' person or work not by mere coincidence but by divine plan.
- *To act as a predictive pattern or resemblance*: the same truth is found in the Old Testament picture and the New Testament fulfillment.
- *Of Jesus' person and work*: the truth in the picture is enlarged, heightened, and clarified in the fulfillment.
- *Or of opposition to both*: God also gave prophetic pictures of Jesus' enemies.

EXAMPLE: The Passover lamb was a type of Jesus. The Passover was a real event. The truths of substitutionary sacrifice and redemption by blood were found in both the type and the anti-type [literally "in place of the type," meaning "fulfillment of the type"]. These truths were enlarged, heightened, and clarified in the fulfillment. The fulfillment was the God-man—not just a lamb; and He redeemed from spiritual and eternal bondage—not just physical and temporary bondage.

With that preliminary understanding of typology, let us now consider questions to help us identify types with confidence and interpret them in a way that unfolds their Christ-centered beauty.

The Picture

First, we want to ask some questions about the type itself:

Is the type real?

Unlike an allegory, which may be fictional (for example, *Pilgrim's Progress*), a type is always a real someone or something. Following are various kinds of types in the Old Testament and an example of each:

- *Person*: Adam, as a representative man, was a type of Jesus.[1]
- *Place*: Jerusalem is a type of the church and also of heaven.[2]
- *Object*: The tabernacle was a type of God's dwelling with men through Jesus and in heaven.[3]
- *Event*: Noah's flood was a picture prophecy of the destruction at the end of the world.[4]
- *Office*: The prophet, the priest, and the king were anointed with oil and typified Jesus, who was anointed with the Holy Spirit to be the greatest prophet, the greatest priest, and the greatest king.[5]

We must emphasize the reality of the types and focus on them to avoid the dangers of mere allegorizing in which the actual Old Testament people and events are rendered largely insignificant while a deeper meaning is sought, a meaning that often has little or no connection with the original historical person or event.

Is the type explicit or implied?

Some types are explicit; the New Testament expressly identifies them as such. Probably due to excessive identification of types by many, some Christian teachers insist that the only legitimate types are those that the Bible explicitly identifies. While understanding their motives, consider these four arguments against this minimizing of biblical types:

- Although typology is prophecy in pictures, no one limits Old Testament prophecy to only what the New Testament explicitly says is a prophecy.
- The Hebrews were rebuked for their slowness in understanding the typology of Melchizedek; yet until then, Melchizedek had not been explicitly identified as a type.[6]
- Limiting ourselves only to explicit types would mean that while minor characters such as Melchizedek and Jonah are types because they are identified as such in the New Testament, major biblical personalities such as Joseph and Joshua are not.
- The aim of the types, which was to prepare God's people for Jesus' coming, could not have been accomplished if the types were limited to the very few explicitly identified as such.[7]

If we use explicit types as examples or specimens, we can identify features, principles, and rules to guide the identification and interpretation of implied types and their fulfillments.

EXAMPLES: The explicit identification of Moses as a type of Jesus in his role as God's appointed mediator and leader of Israel implies the identification of Joshua as a type of Jesus in his similar role as God's appointed mediator and leader of Israel as well.

Also, Scripture refers to the Old Testament ceremonies in

general as "a shadow of the good things to come."[8] It does not explicitly mention every single element of the ceremonies, for example, the showbread, the golden candlestick, and the Feast of Tabernacles. However, the general statement covers the particulars.

THE PRINCIPLES

Having identified a type, we then ask, what were the essential theological truths contained in it?

WHAT WAS THE TYPE DESIGNED TO TEACH THE ORIGINAL AUDIENCE?

One of the most common mistakes in typology is to immediately fast-forward to the fulfillment to help us understand the type. We must remember that the original audience did not have the fulfillment to help them. We must *initially* try to consider the type in isolation from later revelation by asking, what was this type designed to teach the original audience in the original setting? We must try to take the point of view of the original hearers and ask how the type was designed to minister to their needs and edify their souls.

EXAMPLE: The Passover taught the original Israelites the following essential truths: (1) God's anger against sin is severe, (2) God's anger can be turned away by the sacrificial blood of a perfect substitute, (3) God grants safety only to those who are "under" the blood, and (4) God's salvation redeems from bondage.

Many people today are skeptical about how much the Israelites understood of the types. In addition to the Eastern mind-set's being especially attuned to learning through symbols, there are four other factors to bear in mind.

First, there is *the help of previous revelation*. We must not consider the types in isolation from previous revelation. The types were given against a background of accumulating biblical truth. From Genesis 3:15 onward, the expectation and anticipation of a Savior were being continually fostered by God and His servants. However much the people of Israel were reminded of the past and taught for the present, they were always peering over the horizon for the coming Savior, variously known as "the Seed of the woman," "the Seed of Abraham," and "the Son of David." And they used the Old Testament types—person, place, object, event—as spectacles to help them look in the right direction and look for the right person.

Second, we must consider *the assistance of accompanying revelation*. Though there is little in the way of direct explanation of the types by the patriarchs or prophets, we ought not to conclude that there was none. Just because it was not recorded does not mean God did not give it.[9]

Third, they also had *the benefit of practice*. After Sinai, the Israelites were trained in the use of symbolic institutions from their youngest years.

Fourth, the types met *the needs of an infant church*. God recognized that theological truth in *sentence* form would be very difficult for Israelites to grasp. So, He gave theological truth in *sense* form. He gave things Israel could see, hear, touch, smell, and taste. And every sight, sound, touch, smell, and even taste conveyed truth about God's character. Through these prophetic pictures, God was teaching His infant children His spiritual alphabet, and as they slowly put these letters together, they spelled *Jesus*.

What light did later Old Testament revelation cast upon the type?

Just as much of what Christ taught His disciples was not understood by them until later,[10] so the teaching value of each Old Testament type increased with the progress of Old Testament revelation.

EXAMPLE: The Israelites' experience of substitutionary sacrifice at the first Passover would have been far better understood as a type of the ultimate substitutionary sacrifice by later generations of Israelites who had the additional benefit of all the Levitical sacrifices.

As the Old Testament revelation unfolded, the prophets increasingly recognized previous Old Testament events and people as types. Something in the past might be prophesied as going to appear again in the future, even though nothing in the past event of itself gave prophetic indication of the future.

EXAMPLE: In chapters 40–66, Isaiah predicted a far greater exodus in the future, bigger than anything Israel had known before.

As Fairbairn said, the use of the known gave shape and form to the unknown.[11] The images of the past were stamped on the future. The prophets perceived the same essential elements of truth and principle in both the type and the future events but also saw the future was to be a brighter and better exhibition of these same truths and principles. To paraphrase Fairbairn, Old Testament history was pregnant with the seeds of a similar but better future.[12]

What were the inadequacies of the type?

There was an inbuilt inadequacy in the types, which was felt by those who truly understood them. Biblical scholar Vern

Poythress wrote, "The Old Testament thus reaches out in longing for Christ who brings an end to its frustrations and brings to accomplishment its promises."[13]

EXAMPLE: The Passover redeemed from physical bondage but not spiritual bondage; and the sacrifice had to be repeated every year. No lamb was ever totally perfect, and even if such a lamb could have been found, any thinking person would know the impossibility of an irrational creature being an adequate substitute for his intelligent and rational life.

THE PRACTICE

HOW DID AN OLD TESTAMENT BELIEVER USE OR RELATE TO THE TYPES BY FAITH?

How did the more spiritual Old Testament believers use and relate to the types? What role and place did they have in their own lives of faith? Let's consider two answers here:

First, some say that *the types saved those who grasped the essential truths contained in them.* If we take the most obvious Old Testament type, that of sacrifice, some say that as long as the offerer understood and believed the essential truths in the type, he presented an acceptable service to God, regardless of whether or not he saw ahead to the fulfillment. This is Patrick Fairbairn's view, and it's one area where I disagree with him. He argued that to expect an Old Testament believer to see the essential truths in the type *and* what it predicted was too much to ask. He wrote, "[Old Testament sacrifice] had a meaning of its own, which it was possible for the ancient worshipper to understand, and, so understanding, to present through it an acceptable service to

God, whether he might perceive or not the further respect it bore to a dying Savior."[14] I disagree with this position because it minimizes the revealing ability of the type and the enlightening work of the Holy Spirit in the Old Testament believer's life. We also end up with people in heaven who never knew the Messiah until they met Him there.

The second answer, and I believe the correct one, is that *the type saved only those who by faith saw the great future antitype.* While I agree with Fairbairn that the least New Testament believer was more mature than the greatest Old Testament believer,[15] no Old Testament believer was ever saved by understanding merely the essential truths in the types. And while I agree with Fairbairn that "their acceptance as worshippers did not depend on the clearness of their discernment in regard to the person and work of Christ,"[16] they must have had some discernment of Christ to be saved.[17] Poythress argued along similar lines:

> As they looked ahead through the shadows, longing for something better, they took hold on the promises of God that He would send the Messiah. . . . In pictorial form God was saying, as it were, "Look at My provisions for you. This is how I redeem you and bring you to My presence. But look again, and you will see that it is all an earthly symbol of something better. Do not rely on it as if it were the end. Trust Me to save you fully when I fully accomplish My plans." Israelites had genuine communion with God when they responded to what He was saying in the tabernacle. They trusted in the Messiah, without knowing all the details of how fulfillment would finally come. And so they were saved, and they received forgiveness, even before the Messiah came. The animal sacrifices in themselves

did not bring forgiveness (Hebrews 10:1–4), but Christ did as
He met with them through the symbolism of the sacrifices.[18]

THE PERFECTION

Having identified the type with all its essential principles and all
its inadequacies, we now look for the perfect fulfillment of the
type.

ARE BOTH THE TYPE AND THE FULFILLMENT OF THE SAME MORAL QUALITY?

The evil that opposed a type—for example, Goliath opposing David—may have been a type of something similarly evil
that would later oppose the fulfillment—for example, the Devil
opposing the Son of David. Evil actions, however, are never types
of Jesus' person and work. This allows us to decide when a biblical
character is a type of Jesus and when he is not. It is not necessary
to insist that if someone was a type of Jesus at one time in his life,
he was a type in all parts of his life.

EXAMPLES: Jonah was a type of Jesus in his suffering, "death,"
"burial," and "resurrection" and in his preaching of repentance,
which turned many to God.[19] He was not a type in his disobedience to the divine call. Adam is a type of Jesus insofar as he was a
representative man whose actions affected all united to him. He
was not a type in his sin or its evil consequences.[20]

WHAT ARE THE ESSENTIAL RESEMBLANCES?

The foundation of typology is that the same gospel truths
are presented in both Testaments—though presented in different

ways. That is why the Old Testament institutions are called shadows of gospel truths.[21] A shadow implies likeness and resemblance with what casts the shadow.

We are looking for the same truths in both the type and its fulfillment. It is vital, however, to distinguish the *mere external similarities* between the type and its fulfillment from *the essential truths* they share. An outward or superficial resemblance between two objects or persons in the Old and New Testaments does not produce a type-fulfillment relationship. A focus on outward similarity, superficial resemblance, coincidental parallels, and accidental likenesses has often elevated irrelevant likenesses and brought typology into disrepute.

EXAMPLE: For example, although Noah's ark and Jesus' cross were both wooden, that does not in itself produce a type-fulfillment relationship. On the other hand, while Peter told us that the Flood was a type of baptism,[22] apart from the presence of water, there is virtually no outward resemblance between them (Noah and his family were not literally baptized in the flood waters). But there is a deeper resemblance. Just as the Flood destroyed the corrupt from the earth and saved the righteous for a new and better beginning, so baptism signifies (but does not secure) God's gracious work of cleansing the soul from corruption and a new beginning.

DOES THE TYPE PRESENT THE SAME TRUTH IN A SIMPLER WAY?

Just as stepping-stones help us cross to something better by taking small steps, so a type contained the same truth as its fulfillment but in a form that was easier to understand. A type does not say everything there is to say about a truth, but it does say something—something that is true, understandable, and memorable. By putting it in simple picture form, God communicates truth in a more effective way than thousands of scrolls would in Israel's situation.

For example, if a young child were presented with a detailed technical drawing of a plane, he would understand nothing. He might not even see the outline of the plane due to all the overwhelming detail. If the child was presented with a small-scale, simple, outline drawing of a plane, however, then at least he would be able to identify it. He would see the big picture. The child would also benefit from individual separate drawings of the most important parts.

This is why the Mosaic institutions are called the *rudiments* or elementary principles of religious truth and life.[23] They were small-scale, simple, outline drawings of the big spiritual picture with its spiritual and heavenly dimensions. Many parts of the Old Testament institutions also acted as individual separate drawings of the most important elements of salvation.

EXAMPLE: The Passover is a small-scale, simple, outline drawing of the person and work of Jesus. It is easier to understand a spotless lamb than a sinless human nature. It is easier to understand a lamb's death than the death of the Son of God. It is easier to understand the deliverance from physical slavery than deliverance from spiritual bondage.

DOES THE FULFILLMENT PRESENT THE SAME TRUTH ENLARGED, CLARIFIED, AND HEIGHTENED?

When moving from type to fulfillment, there must be a move from the lesser to the greater,[24] from the material to the spiritual, from the earthly to the heavenly. The fulfillment—often called the *antitype*, meaning "type replacement"—presents the same essential truths as the type but

- *enlarged*: The truth, which existed in bud form in the type, comes to full flower under the fulfillment.
- *clarified*: The truth, which previously was partially obscured in the shadows, is made clearer and plainer.
- *heightened*: Although there may be an earthly or external element in the fulfillment, in general it will have a higher and more heavenly nature.

It's as if *gospel* was spelled in a 12-point font in the Old Testament and in a 1200-point in the New Testament. Or we might say it was pictured in the Old using thumbnails but blown up to poster size in the New.

EXAMPLE: In Hebrews 3–4 the Israelites' Canaan rest is compared to the far greater rest of the believer. And the eternal punishment of unbelieving rebels is far greater than the loss of earthly rest.

THE PROGRESS

WHAT EXTRA LIGHT DOES THE NEW TESTAMENT SHED ON THE TYPE?

However much or little Old Testament readers understood the types, New Testament readers can understand them much better with the benefit not only of more revelation but, above all, with the benefit of the coming of the great fulfillment—Jesus Christ. There are two extremes to avoid at this stage:

First, we must avoid the extreme of *only in New Testament light*. Some believe that the types were so shrouded in darkness that only in the light of the New Testament can we see any truth in the types. For example, Sidney Greidanus argues that very few of the types were originally understood as predictive by the original readers or even the writers, but only become so when viewed from the perspective of the New Testament.[25]

While we can agree with Greidanus that Old Testament believers did not see *all* that we see from our New Testament perspective, it is another thing entirely to say that, apart from a few exceptional types such as the Passover, Old Testament believers saw *nothing* predictive of Jesus and the gospel age in the types. If this were true, it is hard to account for the number of types in the Old Testament and the considerable proportion of Old Testament scripture devoted to them.

Second, we must avoid the extreme of *no New Testament light.* While we reject the idea that only New Testament believers had light on the types, we must also reject the denial of New Testament light to help us understand the types. Some are of the view that we must not bring any New Testament knowledge into our consideration of the types, as the original readers did not have this. We are not saying that they did. But we do; and we should use it. Poythress argued along similar lines:

> Having obtained a picture from the original historical circumstances, we are ready to extend the picture and fill it out by seeing how God continues His story and His revelation in the later prophets and in the New Testament. These further reflections may also help us to discriminate better between what is incidental and what is most central in our earlier reflection. We may sometimes correct earlier impressions when we hear more of the story.[26]

EXAMPLE: The New Testament casts further light on the Passover and its antitype not only in the gospel accounts of Christ's sacrifice but also in 1 Corinthians 5:7–8; 1 Peter 1:19; and Revelation 5:6.

WHAT LIGHT DO THE TYPES CAST ON THE NEW TESTAMENT?

In addition to the New Testament casting light on the Old Testament types, the types cast light on the New Testament. While Old Testament types taught Old Testament believers about the Messiah's future person and work, God also designed them to teach New Testament believers lessons about Jesus' person and work—lessons that we could not learn from the New Testament alone.

Also, though we have the great privilege of the fuller New Testament revelation, we are still creatures of sense living in an imperfect spiritual state. It remains difficult for us to grasp heavenly and spiritual truth without the help of some outward physical exhibitions and illustrations of it, such as we have in the Old Testament types.

EXAMPLE: Jonah's thoughts, feelings, and prayers as he descended into the darkest deeps as a result of his sin shed much typological light on Jesus' thoughts, feelings, and prayers as He descended into the darkness of God's anger as a result of His people's sins.[27]

DOES THE TYPE HAVE MORE THAN ONE FULFILLMENT?

Because Jesus is the head of His body, the church, some types may be fulfilled in both Jesus and His people.

EXAMPLE: The anointings of the Old Testament prefigured the work of Jesus and our service to Him. Like Him, we, as Christians, have an anointing from God and function as prophets or forth-tellers of God's Word, priests, and kings.[28]

Typology also helps us interpret the future as well as the past. The future of the Christian church is often described in terms that are borrowed from the Old Testament. It is largely "through the characters, ordinances, and events of the Old Covenant, not those of the New, that the things to come are shadowed forth to the eye of faith."[29]

EXAMPLE: The tabernacle was a type of God's dwelling with men through Jesus but also of God's dwelling with men in heaven for all eternity.[30]

SURFACE DIFFERENCES BUT ESSENTIAL UNITY

On the face of it, there seem to be significant differences between the Old and New Testaments. At times, they seem to portray two different religions. Typology helps us see under these surface differences to the essential unity and identity of gospel truth in both Testaments. It also transforms the book of Psalms into a Christian hymnbook.

But to get the most out of typology, we need a prayerful and humble spirit. There are so few good commentaries on the types, and there is so much room for abusing Scripture and exposing God's Word to ridicule, that we should be extra careful in reading and teaching from these passages. But let's also proceed in faith. God has devoted a large part of His Word to the types, and neglect of them will only impoverish our souls and His church.

CHAPTER 14

CHRIST'S PROMISES

*Discovering Jesus in the Old
Testament Covenants*

From time to time, like all kids, I was too sick to go to school. And as much as I hated school, being at home all day with only three channels of daytime TV (yes, I'm that old) for my only company was almost as bad. One program I did enjoy, though, was an antiques show in which experts would find junk furniture in people's attics or garages, take them to their workshops, then strip, repair, repaint, and recover them before representing them to their shocked owners with an indication of the increased value of the piece. In a very real sense, they had a new piece of furniture with new, higher, and increasing value. And it was all done without their paying a cent. Much better than going to the mall and buying a completely new piece of furniture that decreased in value before they got it home.

That difference between *renewed* and *brand-new* is the gospel key to finding Christ in the Old Testament covenants. It's a key that took me a long time to find and cost me a lot of pain when I did find it.

Some years ago, at fairly short notice, I was asked to speak at a conference in South Africa on the Christ of the covenants. Since I had been completely bamboozled by covenant theology at seminary and had hardly looked at the subject since then, I really should have said, "No. Find someone who knows what he is talking about." However, I was keen to see South Africa, and I had a month or so to prepare six messages. So, off I went, in my youthful zeal, writing out my messages on the Old Testament covenants. With a week to go and the messages almost complete, I thought I should send them to a senior pastor friend who had made a lifetime study of the covenants—yes, I know, I should have asked him to go to South Africa instead.

MY WORLD FALLS APART

Within a few hours, he sent me an alarming e-mail. Ever the gentleman, he wrote, "Dear David, we need to talk. You've portrayed all the Old Testament covenants as legal arrangements where man does his bit and God does His bit. Are you aware that the most common historical position is that these are all covenants of grace where God does everything and man simply receives?" He pointed me to numerous persuasive verses and confessional statements—some of which I had officially subscribed to—and then suggested I read O. Palmer Robertson's *Christ of the Covenants*.

That title rang a bell from seminary days; I looked behind me on the shelf, and there it was. I opened it, and as I read, my world fell apart. Actually my world was about to be transformed for good, but all I could think about was weeks of wasted work and one week left of night-and-day work.

My fundamental mistake had been to take Jeremiah's promise of a *new* covenant to mean that all the previous covenants had been ditched and God was starting something completely new.[1] I learned, however, that God was not promising something completely new; rather He was going to take the old promises, the old covenant promises, and present them in a new and more valuable way.

That's what Jesus was doing when He instituted the sacrament of bread and wine and said: "This cup is the new testament [literally *covenant*] in My blood, which is shed for you."[2] He was deliberately and consciously fulfilling God's promises of a new covenant in Jeremiah 31:31–34. The Greek translation of the Old Testament, the Septuagint, uses *kainos*, the word for "renewed," rather than *neos*, something "brand-new," as do Luke 22:20 and Hebrews 8:13, the New Testament quotations of this passage.[3]

In other words, Jesus was not saying that the old covenant promises should be junked and He was about to start over with a blank slate. He was saying that the old covenant promises were going to be presented in a new, better, and more valuable form. And He was going to do it all Himself without any contribution from us.

That changed my view not only of the new covenant but also of all the Old Testament covenants from Genesis 3 onward. And although I was dreading the prospect of rewriting six addresses, it turned out to be one of the most blessed weeks of work in my life as this gospel key opened up the grace of God in these Old Testament covenants in a way I had never seen before. I went to South Africa with the message of God's unchanging covenant grace in both Testaments, and God richly blessed the messages. I hope you will be blessed, too, as we briefly survey what God taught me that week.

DEFINITION OF A COVENANT

Before we examine these old covenant promises, here's a definition of a divine covenant: *a divine covenant is a relationship, initiated and imposed by a superior, with life-or-death consequences.* There are essentially two kinds of divine covenants in the Bible. In the "covenant of works then wages," God said to Adam in Genesis 2, "If you do this work, then I'll give you these wages." Work, work, work . . . then wages. In contrast, in the "covenant of grace then gratitude," God said, "Here is a great gift for you. Please take it and enjoy it. And here is how to show your gratitude." It is gift, then gratitude.

The covenants with post-fall Adam, Noah, Abraham, Moses, and David were administrations or revelations of the one divine covenant of grace.[4] The promises of the covenant of grace were represented in the form of these covenants. Thus, when Jeremiah prophesied a new covenant, he was not prophesying a new covenant with new parties, terms, and promises. He was prophesying a new administration of the one covenant of grace. The contrast is not with the old covenant of works but with the older administrations or revelations of the one covenant of grace, especially the Mosaic administration of it. Yes, the Mosaic covenant was an administration of the covenant of grace—hang in there.

You might wonder, why didn't God reveal His covenant of grace all at once? Why did He do it in installments? Well, remember that God was working to bring fallen and foolish sinners back into relationship with Him. If He revealed the bright light of His grace all at once, He would have blinded or overwhelmed His creatures. As a wise teacher, He revealed His covenant of grace bit by bit, in phases, simple truths followed by the more complex; and He did this through these Old Testament covenants. These covenants gradually revealed, pictured, and advanced the covenant of grace. As the Westminster Confession of Faith puts it, they "administered" the covenant of grace; they brought it to humanity.[5]

We will be studying the following Old Testament covenants:

- the covenant with Adam: the covenant of the defeated serpent[6]
- the covenant with Noah: the covenant of the disarmed bow[7]
- the covenant with Abraham: the covenant of the knife[8]
- the covenant with Moses: the covenant of lamb and law[9]
- the covenant with David: the covenant of the everlasting king[10]
- the promise and fulfillment of the new covenant[11]

And we will be looking at six features these covenants have in common, six features or characteristics that reveal and administer the covenant of grace. Some features are more obvious in some covenants than others, and some are implicit rather than explicit.

THE SIN

The first thing we notice about these covenant promises is that they take place in the context of sin, emphasizing that God's mercy, not human merit, is the bedrock foundation of His covenant dealings with humanity.

THE COVENANT OF THE DEFEATED SERPENT

This is not the place to prove that the arrangements in Genesis 3:14–15 were covenantal in nature. I refer you to Old Testament scholar O. Palmer Robertson's *Christ of the Covenants* for a convincing argument in favor of this idea.[12] To put it simply, just as a story about a mom, a dad, and their kids is a story about a family, even if the word *family* never appears, so this relationship—initiated and imposed by a superior, with life-or-death consequences—is a covenant, even if the word itself does not appear.

The covenant with Adam was announced immediately after the first sin of our first parents. Instead of walking away from this disaster and instead of wiping out the sinful world and its sinful inhabitants, God promised, or covenanted, to reverse the effects of this first sin and restore His perfect order.

THE COVENANT OF THE DISARMED BOW

God announced the covenant with Noah immediately after the judgment of a worldwide deluge, just before Noah fell into the most degrading sins, and in the full knowledge of the evil heart of man.[13] Yet in His grace and mercy, God promised that He would never drown the whole world again. He promised that He would not deal with human life on this earth according to their sins.

THE COVENANT OF THE KNIFE

The covenant with Abraham, with its promise of a miraculous son, was announced by God even when He knew that Abraham would so soon turn his back on the divine promise and seek a son by sinful means.[14]

THE COVENANT OF LAMB AND LAW

God announced the covenant with Moses not long after Israel had sinned in connection with both bread and water, and a short time before Israel's sin with the golden calf.[15]

THE COVENANT OF THE EVERLASTING KING

The covenant with David was announced with God's full knowledge that David would soon commit adultery and murder. David himself saw the grace of God in this when, on his death-bed, he reflected on how his sins had shattered his own family, and yet God's covenant promises remained "sure."[16]

THE NEW COVENANT

Jeremiah 31:31–34 predicted a new covenant for Israel on the eve of their exile in Babylon on account of their sins, especially the sins of their covenant breaking.[17] Jesus Himself announced the fulfillment of the new covenant on the eve of His exile for the sins of His own spiritual Israel.[18]

SUMMARY

One of the essential truths revealed by these Old Testament covenant promises is that God is gracious, that God covenants with men and women not according to their merits but according to His mercy. God met every broken promise of humanity with a new promise of grace from heaven.

JESUS ON EVERY PAGE

THE START

We have gained many insights into the biblical covenants by the discovery of covenant documents from biblical times and cultures. As we noted in chapter 12, these covenants have been called *suzerain-vassal treaties*. The big king (a suzerain) detailed all he had done for the little king (a vassal) before setting out rules to ensure the relationship would be happy and healthy. The document usually concluded with the suzerain encouraging the vassal to thankful obedience with promises of reward and threats for disobedience.

This type of suzerain-vassal treaty is seen to greater or lesser degrees in God's Old Testament covenants, where God is the Suzerain and humanity is the vassal. God designs and dictates the terms of the covenant. It is not a mutual agreement but a sovereign imposition, which humanity rejects at its peril. It is God, not man, who initiates it. And God's benevolence is stated before stipulating what God expects in grateful response.

THE COVENANT OF THE DEFEATED SERPENT

God sovereignly announced the terms of this covenant when He came into the garden of Eden after our first parents' first sin. Adam and Eve were in no position to bargain. God took the initiative, however, and promised grace to them when they had nothing to give Him. Notice the great "I will" as He stepped in to break up the unholy "friendship" between the Devil and humanity: "I will put enmity . . ."[19]

THE COVENANT OF THE DISARMED BOW

The covenant with Noah begins: "As for Me, behold, I establish

My covenant with you . . ."[20] If you look at this and the surrounding verses, you see again and again the divine initiative underlined: "I will establish . . . I make . . . I set . . . I will remember . . . I have established . . ." As in all the covenants between God and man, God is the Giver and man the receiver.

THE COVENANT OF THE KNIFE

In the covenant with Abraham, God took the initiative in the midst of Abraham's fears and impotence: "Fear not, Abram [later Abraham]: I am thy shield, and thy exceeding great reward."[21] God made the promises, and Abraham received and believed them.[22]

THE COVENANT OF LAMB AND LAW

Moses was confronted with God's sovereign initiative and success before he heard any words of law: "You have seen what I did [divine deeds] to the Egyptians, and how I bore you on eagles' wings [divine deliverance] and brought you to Myself [divine destiny]. Now therefore. . . ."[23] The Ten Commandments also begin not with human effort but with the divine initiative.[24]

THE COVENANT OF THE EVERLASTING KING

The covenant with David came closest to a divine-human negotiation or deal. David came with a proposal to God, to build Him a house. But God swept David's initiative and ideas aside and imposed His own arrangement, which far transcended anything David had in mind. Instead of David's idea of building a temporary physical house for God, God would build David an everlasting house—meaning dynasty—for His own glory and the good of humanity.[25]

The New Covenant

To see the divine initiative in the new covenant promised by Jeremiah, we need only quote Jeremiah 31:33: "This is the covenant that I will make with the house of Israel after those days, says the LORD: I will put My law in their minds, and write it on their hearts; and I will be their God, and they shall be My people."

This divine initiative is seen in an unparalleled way when Jesus fulfilled the new covenant promise. "When the fulness of the time was come, God sent forth his Son, made of a woman, made under the law, to redeem them that were under the law, that we might receive the adoption of sons."[26]

Summary

One of the essential principles revealed by these covenants is that God takes the sovereign initiative in His covenant dealings with men and women. He took the first step toward mankind in his weakness and helplessness. Indeed, He took the ultimate step of self-sacrifice.

The Sacrifice

God's covenants are also usually instituted with bloodshed, indicating the life-or-death seriousness of the relationship.

The Covenant of the Defeated Serpent

The covenant with Adam promises a bruising or crushing of the Devil's head, and this promise of bloodshed is immediately followed by the killing of animals to provide coats for Adam and Eve and the practice of divinely approved sacrifice in the very next chapter.[27]

THE COVENANT OF THE DISARMED BOW

Noah and his family began life in a fresh, new world with fresh covenant promises and multiple sacrifices.[28]

THE COVENANT OF THE KNIFE

To ratify a covenant, it was customary in that day for the contracting parties in an agreement to walk between the pieces of slain animals. When the parties walked between the pieces, they were saying that if they failed to keep their word, they deserved the same fate as the animals—to be torn in pieces.[29]

In the covenant with Abraham, God alone, in a theophany—literally, God-appearance—of smoke and fire, walked between the pieces.[30] God alone ratified the covenant. God alone accepted all the covenant obligations. God alone took upon Him the solemn oaths and imprecations should He fail. As we shall see, there was a further cutting and sacrifice of human blood when God gave Abraham the additional and more permanent covenant sign of circumcision after his sin with Hagar.

THE COVENANT OF LAMB AND LAW

The Ten Commandments conclude with a reference to sacrifice.[31] Pages and pages of law concerning sacrifices follow the Ten Commandments. The Mosaic covenant inauguration was concluded in Exodus 24 by Moses sprinkling them with the blood of the covenant.[32]

THE COVENANT OF THE EVERLASTING KING

If the Davidic kings sinned, God promised their blood would have to be shed at the hands of other men.[33] This sacrifice of their blood would again underline the life-or-death nature of divine covenants and the connection between sin and bloodshed.

The New Covenant

The prediction of the new covenant does not have any explicit sacrificial reference. When Jesus announced His fulfillment of the new covenant, however, the sacrificial emphasis was made crystal clear: "This cup is the new covenant in My blood, which is shed for you."[34]

Summary

One of the essential truths revealed by these covenants is that God requires sacrificial blood to atone for sin and that such sacrifice was at the foundation of covenant relationships. These Old Testament covenants revealed and advanced the covenant of grace, in which God not only declared the requirement of sacrifice but also provided it—indeed became it.

The Speech

Although the covenants were multifaceted, one dominant truth was usually communicated, which met a particular need at that time.

The Covenant of the Defeated Serpent

In the covenant with defeated Adam, the dominant truth was victory. Despite the opposition and minor triumphs of the Devil, God would ensure ultimate victory over him and his seed.

The Covenant of the Disarmed Bow

After God's declaration of war on the world and the tumult of the worldwide flood, God promised peace. He assured nervous

Noah that He would provide a relatively peaceful and predictable environment.[35]

THE COVENANT OF THE KNIFE

Since Abraham's great need was a son, Abraham was promised a seed as numerous as the stars of heaven and a land where they would live.[36]

THE COVENANT OF LAMB AND LAW

Moses was facing a seemingly impossible task. The great exodus redemption had left him as leader of an unruly and disorganized multitude. Authoritative law was the need, and God's law was the provision.[37]

THE COVENANT OF THE EVERLASTING KING

God chose David to be His king over Israel. As David well knew, however, kings and kingdoms came and went all the time. Therefore God promised David an everlasting king and an everlasting kingdom.

THE NEW COVENANT

As the new covenant was announced in the context of judgment for Israel's sin, it promised forgiveness and cleansing. When Jesus announced the fulfillment of the new covenant, He also connected it with the "remission of sins."[38]

SUMMARY

The essential themes of these Old Testament covenants were victory, peace, a son, obedience, a king, and forgiveness. These Old Testament covenants revealed and advanced the covenant of grace in which Jesus conquers the Devil, Jesus is our peace, Jesus is the promised Son, Jesus secures obedience to God, Jesus is the everlasting King, and Jesus forgives our sins by His blood.

THE SIGN

God not only gave word promises in these covenants; He also gave picture promises, which served as simpler and more permanent reminders of the divine covenants.

THE COVENANT OF THE DEFEATED SERPENT

To underline the promise of victory, Adam was given the covenant sign of a disgraced and defeated serpent—cursed above all animals, in the lowest place, eating dust.

THE COVENANT OF THE DISARMED BOW

To emphasize the promise of peace, Noah was given the covenant seal of the beautiful storm-concluding rainbow.

THE COVENANT OF THE KNIFE

To help Abraham remember the promise of a son, he was given the sign of circumcision, a sign engraved in his own flesh. What a reminder, not only of the blood-filled consequences of his sin, but also of God's commitment to fulfill His covenant promises through the physical seed of Abraham.

THE COVENANT OF LAMB AND LAW

Moses was given two covenant signs—the lamb and the law. And it is vital to note the order: the lamb came before the law. Passover night in Egypt came before the chiseling of the law at

Mount Sinai, the first revealing God's provision, and the second how God's people should respond to that provision.

The Covenant of the Everlasting King

The crown on David's head reminded him and all Israel of God's promise of an everlasting king and kingdom.

The New Covenant

The new covenant signs are the bread and the wine, signifying the body and the blood given to secure our forgiveness.[39]

Summary

The covenant signs accompanied and confirmed the verbal promises. The defeated snake promised the future Seed's victory over the Devil. The rainbow promised a Seed who would make peace with God. The knife of circumcision promised a Seed from the line of Abraham. The lamb and the law promised a Seed who would redeem and bring into holy relationship with God. The crown promised the Seed's everlasting throne and rule. The bread and the wine promised forgiveness through the Seed's broken body and shed blood.

The Scope

Here we consider the scope of the Old Testament covenants. We ask, who were the beneficiaries? Who came within the scope of these covenants? The answer, as we shall see, is that the covenants had a double scope. There were external, physical, and nonredemptive blessings for a great many, in some cases for all humanity. And there were internal, spiritual, and redemptive blessings for those who, by faith, saw through the externals of the covenants to the spiritual realities they represented.

The Covenant of the Defeated Serpent

Imagine a large cathedral with no windows and no doors. Inside this black and bleak building is fallen humanity. In mercy, God cuts a small snake-shaped window in one wall to let in a little light from the covenant of grace. Everyone inside benefited from the light, just as all humanity benefited from God's curse on the dangerous snake. However, though many just admire the shape of the window and enjoy the light that comes through it, together with its natural benefits, others look through the window by faith and see a welcome spiritual reality shining brightly through it—the defeated Devil of the covenant of grace.

The Covenant of the Disarmed Bow

In the covenant with Noah, God cut another cathedral window, this time rainbow shaped. Just as everyone inside gets more light, so everyone profits from the promised benefits of a generally stable cycle of seasons. Again, some just take the physical light and climatic benefits, and some just admire the window. Others, however, look through the window by faith and see a more wonderful spiritual reality shining brightly through it—a peacemaking and pacified God.

The Covenant of the Knife

Some years later, God cut a knife-shaped window. This time the light that shines through is confined to the natural descendants of Abraham and those associated with them by circumcision of the male family members. All the natural descendants of Abraham benefit from God's promises of seed and land, together with His promise to bless and curse other nations according to their treatment of Abraham and his descendants. Again, some just take the benefits of the natural light, and some just admire the window.[40] Others, however, look through the window by faith and see the provision of a Savior physically descended from Abraham, who would be cut off for sin, to ensure that His people would be cut off from their sin.[41]

THE COVENANT OF LAMB AND LAW

God cut two more windows just for Israel, one lamb shaped and the other scroll shaped—the law. All in Israel reap national and physical benefits from God's redemption of the nation from Egypt, His special relationship with that nation, and His promised blessings upon their obedience. Again, some just take the benefits of the natural light, and some just admire the lamb- and scroll-shaped windows. Others, however, look through the windows by faith and see personal, spiritual, and redemptive benefits shining brightly through them.

THE COVENANT OF THE EVERLASTING KING

The crown-shaped window, representing God's special relationship to the Davidic monarchy, brought many external, though nonredemptive, blessings to Israel. Again, some just take the benefits of the natural light, and some just admire the window. Others, however, look through the window by faith and see something far better and higher shining brightly through it: the divine provision of a Son of David who would spiritually deliver and internally rule them forever.

THE NEW COVENANT

In the new covenant God punched huge holes all over the cathedral walls in order to flood in unprecedented light from the covenant of grace. Some holes are shaped like loaves of broken bread and cups of red wine—the Lord's Supper. There are also fountain-shaped holes—baptism. These New Testament signs of the covenant of grace declare the grace of the gospel to all nations (not just Israel) in an unparalleled manner. It is as if God says, "I cannot make My provision of an unconditional salvation any clearer than this." Though some still prefer the shadows, and some still simply admire the windows, innumerable sin-darkened souls flock to the light coming through the new sign-windows and trace the new covenant signs of bread and wine to what they signify: a crucified Savior bleeding, bruised, and broken for sin and for sinners. And they trace the new covenant sign of baptismal water to what it signifies: forgiveness and cleansing from sin. Those who sit in darkness see a great light.

We await one final development in the unfolding plan of God: the return of Jesus for His people. Then He will demolish the cathedral, its walls and windows: "I saw no temple therein: for the Lord God Almighty and the Lamb are the temple of it. And the city had no need of the sun, neither of the moon, to shine in it: for the glory of God did lighten it, and the Lamb is the light thereof."[42] Then the essence of the covenant of grace will be fully realized and experienced: "He will dwell with them, and they shall be His people. God Himself will be with them and be their God."[43] Then we will hear the divine voice say forever: "I will be his God and he shall be My son."[44]

Summary

The covenants reveal God's wide scope in His widespread offer of covenant benefits, even though comparatively few actually use the covenant benefits in the right way—to believe in the Christ of the covenants.

What's New?

At this point, you are probably asking, as I did, "If there is so much that is 'old' in the new covenant, what's new? If there is so much continuity between the old and new covenants, is there any difference, any discontinuity?" And the answer is yes, there is much that is new. The new covenant exceeds the old covenant in the following ways:

New Universality

From Abraham on, God's covenants had been narrowed down to Abraham's descendants, then to Israel, then to David's sons for Israel's benefit. But in the new covenant, there is a new international emphasis. Jesus said, "Go therefore and make disciples of all the nations."[45]

New Personality

In the old administrations of the covenant of grace, Jesus and His grace were promised and pictured. In the new covenant, Jesus is fully and personally present. The pictures and ceremonies are gone, and the Jesus of the pictures and ceremonies is present. It is the difference between reading a biography of a person and actually meeting the person. In the new covenant the words on the page come alive: "The Word was made flesh and dwelt among us . . . full of grace and truth."[46]

NEW CLARITY

When we see a shadow coming around a corner, we have a rough idea of what is casting the shadow. However, sometimes the reality can be quite different. The shadow reveals, but the shadow also obscures. In the new covenant, Jesus has come around the corner, and we see Him far more clearly. Shadows give way to sunshine, prophecy gives way to fulfillment, type gives way to antitype, and symbols give way to reality.

NEW IMMEDIACY

When God made the Old Testament covenants, He usually made them with one person who represented many more people. We might call that representative a steward, one through whom God administered the covenant. God dealt with His people and spoke to them through this covenant head or mediator. However, in the new covenant all sinful and imperfect human intermediaries are swept aside, and the covenant of grace is administered directly and immediately by Jesus. He promises, "I will be your prophet, priest, king, and husband."[47] He acts as the one for the many.[48]

NEW EFFECTIVENESS

Though some, perhaps many, were saved under the older promises and pictures of the covenant of grace, one thing is sure: far more are saved in the new covenant phase of the covenant of grace. So, Jeremiah is not contrasting a new covenant of grace with an old covenant of works. He is contrasting a new and more effective presentation of the covenant of grace with an older but less effective presentation of the same covenant of grace.[49]

NEW SPIRITUALITY

Previous administrations of the covenant of grace, especially the Mosaic administration, were so encumbered with external elements and ceremonies as to be comparatively carnal. The new covenant is more spiritual, more focused on the inward life. The covenants in both Testaments reveal a God who desires relationship with His people, a desire that finds ultimate spiritual satisfaction only through Jesus Christ.

NEW FINALITY

The presentations of the covenant of grace through the mini-covenants of the Old Testament were preparatory and temporary. The new covenant is the final presentation of the covenant of grace in this present world. It will give way only to the eternal enjoyment of the covenant relationship in the new heaven and new earth. And that's what covenant is all about: relationship.

All the Old Testament covenants consistently present a God who seeks relationship with fallen sinners. The new covenant promises also have relationship at their very core. Jeremiah conveyed God's words: "I will be their God, and they shall be My people. No more shall every man teach his neighbor, and every man his brother, saying, 'Know the LORD,' for they all shall know Me, from the least of them to the greatest of them."[50] Jesus was the fulfillment of this covenant promise.[51] He is Immanuel, "God with us."[52] He brings His people into a saving relationship with God. And He will ultimately perfect that relationship too:

"Behold, the tabernacle of God is with men, and He will dwell with them, and they shall be His people. God Himself will be with them and be their God. And God will wipe away every tear from their eyes; there shall be no more death, nor sorrow, nor crying. There shall be no more pain, for the former things have passed away." Then He who sat on the throne said, "Behold, I make all things new."[53]

CHAPTER 15

CHRIST'S PROVERBS

*Discovering Jesus in the Old
Testament Proverbs*

The book of Proverbs is the Old Testament's Twitter. After some introductory chapters that present wisdom's beauty, benefits, and beckonings, we encounter hundreds and hundreds of Tweets—short, pithy, and memorable statements and observations that communicate the most profound theological and practical truths.

But can Jesus be found in these Tweets? It wasn't immediately obvious to me, and it wasn't obvious even after many years of study. That's why I left this chapter until near the end of this book. However, I kept coming back to my foundational confidence in Jesus, who told us that He may be found in *all* the Scriptures.[1] Proverbs is part of "the word of Christ,"[2] through which He reveals Himself to needy sinners.

Although by the very nature of these short verses we tend to be immediately drawn into close and detailed study of them, we first need to step back and take a satellite view of the Old Testament's message. From that eye in the sky, we see that the cumulative message of the Old Testament is that a Savior is coming who will be God's greatest king, God's greatest priest, and God's greatest prophet. And Proverbs majors in that last category.

Some parts of the Old Testament reveal sinners crying out for a king to bring order to their unruly lives. Other parts reveal sinners looking for a priest to forgive their sins. But some sections reveal sinners searching for a teacher to disperse their ignorance and errors and to help them think, believe, speak, and do rightly.

God's greatest Old Testament answer to this deep need is Proverbs, a divinely inspired revelation of wisdom written largely by Solomon, then the wisest man in the world. And yet, like all God's Old Testament answers, this one was temporary, provisional, preparatory, and prophetic of His greatest revelation of wisdom in Jesus Christ. As Jesus said, "A greater than Solomon is here."[3]

Yes, He is here. But He was also there, in Proverbs. And the key to finding Him there is first of all to go backward, to rewind to the giving of the law of Moses. Then we'll hit "Pause" and look at Jesus in Proverbs itself, before fast-forwarding to see the way Jesus and the other New Testament authors reflect on Proverbs.

REWIND

The Proverbs don't just land in the middle of the Old Testament like some unexpected aliens from outer space. No, they grow out of Exodus 20. They take the general principles of God's Law, the Ten Commandments, and give them eyes, ears, hands, and feet. The Law comes alive in the Proverbs as we see what obedience to the Law looks like in daily life—in the home, in business, in relationships, and so on. They flesh out the general principles of the Law in the specifics of everyday life, preparing the way for the literal fleshing out of God's law in Jesus' earthly life.

That relationship between Proverbs and God's law allows us to apply the same ten principles that we used to discover Jesus in His precepts to also find and enjoy Jesus in His proverbs.

An Exhibition of Christ's Character

When we read the book of Proverbs, which describes holiness, wisdom, goodness, mercy, and so forth, we cannot avoid thinking of how these characteristics are found to an infinitely perfect degree in all three persons of the Godhead—the Father, the Son, and the Holy Spirit.

An Exposition of Jesus' Life

Every proverb that commands and commends wise and righteous living effectively expounds Jesus' life on earth. For example, when Jesus rebuked Peter for his spiritual insensitivity and experienced Judas's betrayal, He was experiencing a painful exposition of this proverb:

> *Open rebuke is better*
> *Than love carefully concealed.*
> *Faithful are the wounds of a friend,*
> *But the kisses of an enemy are deceitful.*[4]

When we read the numerous proverbs that describe a holy tongue, we read about the only perfect tongue since Genesis 3, that of Jesus Christ.

An Example of Jesus' Teaching

As Jesus planted the seeds of His future teaching in Proverbs, we shouldn't be surprised to find Him picking up these seeds in His teaching ministry and growing them into fuller flower.

For example, Jesus took the principle in this statement—"Do not boast about tomorrow, for you do not know what a day may bring forth"[5]—and enhanced and expanded it in the Sermon on the Mount.[6] Also, Jesus clarified and sharpened time and again the repeated proverbial challenge to choose between the two paths of folly or wisdom. Old Testament scholars Raymond Dillard and Tremper Longman wrote these challenging words:

> Thus, as Christians read the book of Proverbs in the light of the continued revelation of the New Testament, they are confronted with the same questions as the ancient Israelites, but with a different nuance. Will we dine with Wisdom or with Folly? The Wisdom who beckons us is none other than Jesus Christ, while the folly that attempts to seduce us is any created thing that we put in place of the Creator (Rom. 1:22–23).[7]

An Examination in Jesus' Light

Just as the holy light of Jesus shines through the Ten Commandments, helping us to discover our sins of life and heart, so the holy light of Jesus shines through the specific proverbs. If the Ten Commandments are like ten blinding spotlights, the proverbs are like hundreds of burning lasers, targeting our sins more specifically and painfully. And like the spotlights, the point of the lasers is not to turn us into a bunch of legalistic do-gooders. It is to show us that we are no-gooders, that there is only one Good, and that is God.

An Explanation of Jesus' Death

Like the Law, Proverbs not only demonstrates the *need* for Jesus' death but also explains the *nature* of it. Proverbs vividly describes the typical kind of human scheming and plotting that characterized Jesus' crucifiers.[8] The proverbs deepen our understanding of the Law's curse that was heaped upon Jesus, and they demonstrate the divine principles of penal justice that He would experience in His body and soul.[9]

The Extent of Jesus' Death

Just as the Law demonstrated God's concern with the effects of sin on the whole creation, so Proverbs is taken up with the great things and the small things of life, from royal matters to animal matters, proving again the Lord's wide-angled concern to reorder and renew His whole creation.[10]

The Execution of Jesus' Judgment

By making clear and constant connections between sin and God's punishment of it, Proverbs presents foretastes and warnings of Jesus' final judgment on sin.[11]

The Enjoyment of Jesus' Presence

Just as the Law connects obedience with the blessing and presence of God, and disobedience with cursing and exile from God, Proverbs repeatedly contrasts the blessings of obedience with the losses resulting from disobedience in every area of life—mental, emotional, physical, and spiritual.[12]

An Entrance into Jesus' Home

By painting vivid contrasts between the houses of the wicked and the righteous, Proverbs also gives an insight to the heavenly "house" that Jesus is enjoying right now and that He is also preparing for the righteous.[13] The righteous life and society envisaged by Proverbs make the believer yearn for the perfection of that condition and place that will be enjoyed only in the new heaven and new earth wherein dwell the righteous and righteousness.

The Exaltation of Jesus' Glory

As the Law exalts Jesus in believers' hearts by showing us our need of Him and the perfection of His obedience, so Proverbs' deep and wide exposition and application of the Law make us despair of self-salvation and delight in Jesus' salvation. They make us exalt and value Him more and more for His perfect law keeping and law suffering. And to the extent that He enables us to put His proverbs into practice in our daily lives, we are enabled to exalt and honor Him by our obedience.

Pause

Having rooted the book of Proverbs in the Law, do we now fast-forward to the New Testament to see how Jesus fulfilled the Law and Proverbs? Not so fast. Let's just pause for a few minutes and look a bit more at the book of Proverbs itself, because Jesus is not only predicted there but also present there.

Remember, Old Testament believers read their Bible to find out about the Savior, just as we do. What then did they find out about Him in the book of Proverbs? If they expected a Creator from Genesis; an Emancipator from Exodus; a Priest and a Sacrifice from Leviticus; a Guide from Numbers; a Covenanter from Deuteronomy; a Captain from Joshua; a Judge from Judges; a Redeemer from Ruth; a King from Samuel, Kings, and Chronicles; a Rebuilder from Ezra and Nehemiah; an Innocent Sufferer from Job; and a Worship Leader from Psalms, what did they expect from reading Proverbs?

They expected Mr. Wisdom. The book of Proverbs showed them their ignorance, error, and folly and made them cry out for the wisdom of God that's portrayed in various ways in it.

A Wise Son

One-third of the book of Proverbs contains a father's addresses and appeals to his son. Israel would have read this not merely as King Solomon's words to his royal sons but as God's words to His national son, Israel. The nation, of course, was far from being a faithful and loyal son to its God and Father, but Proverbs surely held out the prospect of someone who would come and fill that role perfectly.[14]

A Wise Teacher

Lady Wisdom is the mediator of God's wisdom.[15] She calls sinners on God's behalf, teaches them in God's name, and points them to God for everything. Her concern to have every detail and particular of Israel's life ordered by God's Word reveals the Lord's love for His church in providing the specifics of how to live in a way that pleases Him.

And yet how painfully the Israelites must have felt the jarring disconnect between Solomon's wise words and Solomon's foolish life. How they must have longed for a wise teacher who would mediate God's knowledge to them in a way that was consistent with their lives.

A Wise Host

When Lady Wisdom saw that Madame Folly had prepared a fatal banquet for the foolish, she prepared her own feast and countered with a gracious invitation.[16] That this was to portray the heart of God for sinners is confirmed by later prophets who picked up this picture and used it to portray God as the divine host calling sinners to fellowship with Him at His dinner table, just as Jesus did on earth.[17]

A Wise Creator

The Israelites knew that God created the world. What they didn't know was the central role that God's Son had in it—that is, until Proverbs 8 was written. It's much easier for us to read Proverbs 8 and see Jesus in it because we have the benefit of John 1:1–4 and Hebrews 1:1–2. In the absence of such clarifying revelation, though, what did the Israelites understand when they read Proverbs 8:22–28?

First, the context is of Lady Wisdom crying out to all who will hear.[18] As we've noted, the Israelites were already expecting the future Savior to be God's final word of wisdom. But then verses 22–28 take us backward, not forward. It's as if Solomon was saying, "Don't just enjoy Wisdom's present role in our nation, and don't just look forward to Wisdom's future role in our salvation. Look back and remember Wisdom's past role in creation." This passage taught Israel these truths:

- Wisdom's distinct identity from the Father
- Wisdom's essential unity with the Father
- Wisdom's eternal existence
- Wisdom's role in the creation of everything

- Wisdom's joy in God's presence
- Wisdom's joy in the creation
- Wisdom's joy in humanity

As commentator William Arnot said, "One might profitably put the question to himself, if the Spirit designed to make known something of the personal history of Christ before His coming, how could He have done so in plainer terms than this chapter contains?"[19]

Unfortunately some translations of Proverbs 8:22–28 suggest that Wisdom was created by God, leading many to think that this cannot be the eternal Son of God. Accurate translations of the Hebrew, however, communicate Wisdom's eternal preexistence, preventing this misunderstanding.

He is portrayed as creating the world and longing for its redemption. We see a triple delight here: the Father's delight in the Son, the Son's delight in the Father, and the Son's delight in the scene and subjects of His redemption.

It's incredible to think that He who was the delight of His Father and delighting in the Father should also find delight in men and women, boys and girls. He longed to be with us, thrilled at the prospect, and anticipated it joyfully. Though He knew how we would treat Him, He loved us and delighted in us.

A Wise Bridegroom

Proverbs 31 is often used to teach about the qualities of a godly woman, and rightly so. Remember, however, that the original Israelite readers of Proverbs were in a covenant relationship with God, a relationship often portrayed as a marriage—even by Solomon in his Song.

Israelite readers of this chapter would, to some extent, read chapter 31 as a description of how the Lord viewed them and of the "bride" He called them to be. Who could not but admire such a loving Bridegroom and long for an even greater revelation of Him and even closer relationship with Him?

Fast-Forward

The Old Testament leaves us looking and longing for the Wise One who would fulfill the Law and Proverbs. No surprise then that Jesus Christ exactly fit that profile. Time and again, Jesus is not only portrayed as *the* wise man but also identified with the wisdom of God.[20] Truly, a greater than Solomon is here.

We can't be sure how much Jesus consciously fulfilled the Old Testament models of the Messiah. Did it come naturally and instinctively to Him, or did He have to work out who He was and then shape His life and character around this? There's more than one verse in Scripture that indicates He took certain actions because He knew that it was an Old Testament expectation. This, of course, doesn't mean He did anything that went against His essential character or He felt forced to be and do anything. It does indicate, however, that Jesus read His Bible to inform and shape His ministry, His method, and the matter of His teaching.

His Ministry

As He read Proverbs, Jesus must have been deeply influenced by the expectation of the Wise One. He was indeed the

Wise Son who pleased His Father in every area of life. He was the Wise Teacher whose unparalleled words of wisdom have stood the test of time. He was the Wise Host who invited weary, hungry, and thirsty outcasts to His gospel banquet and who also promised us a never-ending feast above.[21] He is the Wise Creator, who demonstrated His goodwill toward and delight in humanity throughout His whole earthly life.[22] And He was—and is—the Wise Bridegroom looking for an undeserving wife.[23]

His Manner

Even the manner of Jesus' teaching seems to have been consciously shaped by the book of Proverbs.[24] The Hebrew root of *proverb, mashal,* means "to be like," reminding us of one of the most common ways Jesus introduced His teaching and His parables: "The kingdom of heaven is like . . ." He also specialized in short, pithy, memorable sayings, many of which are part of popular culture to this day.

His Matter

In the Sermon on the Mount, His first public sermon, Jesus quotes from or alludes to Proverbs numerous times—someone counted seven times in the first thirty verses. And He ended that first sermon by calling people to be like the wise man who built his house on the rock.[25]

The ethical continuity between the Old and New Testaments is also seen in the frequency with which Jesus' apostles quote and echo the Proverbs—up to thirty-five times according to some estimates.[26]

PROVERBS INCARNATE

The greater Solomon is here—greater in holiness, greater in glory, greater in power, and far greater in wisdom. Let us worship His wisdom, let us hear His wise teaching, let us be made wise unto salvation, and let us live wisely to His glory and honor.

CHAPTER 16

CHRIST'S POETS

*Discovering Jesus in the Old
Testament Poems*

His planet, His people, His presence, His precepts, His past, His prophets, His pictures, His promises, His proverbs—Jesus comes to us in so many and such varied ways throughout the Old Testament. We should not be surprised that He also comes to us through His Old Testament poets.

In this chapter, we will look at Jesus in the Psalms, a relatively uncontroversial subject,[1] then at Jesus in the Song of Solomon, which, in contrast, has been a much-debated subject over the years.

JESUS IN THE PSALMS

Let's look at some ways we find Jesus in the Psalms:

• We sing *to* Jesus with the Psalms.

- We sing *of* Jesus in the Psalms.
- We sing *with* Jesus in the Psalms.

WE SING TO JESUS WITH THE PSALMS

We must learn to sing the Psalms with trinitarian tongues. That means that when we address God or sing of Him, we are worshipping not just God in general or the Father in particular but the Son of God and the Spirit of God also. When we sing to our Shield, our Rock, our Shepherd, our Judge, our Refuge, our Fortress, our Creator, our Healer, our Provider, or our Redeemer, we sing to all three persons of the Godhead, all equal in power and glory.[2]

Think of how we can use the different kinds of psalms to praise Jesus. We use the psalms of lament to confess our sins to Jesus. We sing the psalms of praise to celebrate Jesus' person and work. We sing the psalms of remembrance to look back on Jesus' acts throughout redemptive history. We sing the psalms of confidence to express our faith in Jesus' salvation. We sing the wisdom psalms to acknowledge that Jesus is our only source of wisdom. We sing the psalms of thanksgiving to express our gratitude for Jesus' daily grace in our times of need.

WE SING OF JESUS IN THE PSALMS

Almost every evangelical agrees that Jesus is in the Psalms to some extent. The question is, to what extent? How many psalms are messianic? How many psalms speak of Jesus in particular?

Some say none and explain away all the psalms' references to "the king" as being an ordinary king of Israel. Others say that although the royal psalms were originally intended to refer to an ordinary king of Israel, later editors organized the material to promote the idea of a future messianic King. Still others go a bit further and say that although most of the psalms were about ordinary kings from David's family, some of them—fifteen or so—do seem to predict a more messianic figure in the future.

You probably won't be surprised if I suggest that we turn away from many of the scholars and take the testimony of the New Testament as our most reliable guide for interpreting the Old Testament. There, Jesus referred to the whole Old Testament as being fulfilled in Himself and specifically pointed to the Psalms, without any qualification or limitation.[3]

Statistics. Old Testament scholar and pastor Derek Kidner draws attention to the fact that although the New Testament explicitly references only fifteen psalms as messianic, closer study of the numerous allusions to Jesus in the Psalms reveals these fifteen as "samples of a much larger corpus." He goes on: "It would scarcely seem too much to infer from this treatment that wherever David or the Davidic King appears in the Psalter . . . he foreshadows in some degree the Messiah."[4]

Consider these further statistics to support a Christ-centered approach to the Psalms:

- The New Testament quotes from the Psalter more often than from any other Old Testament book.
- Of the 283 direct quotes of the Old Testament in the New, 116 (41 percent) are from the Psalms.[5]
- The Psalms are used more than fifty times in the Gospels to allude to the person and work of Jesus Christ.[6]
- When the author of Hebrews sought biblical proof that Jesus was God, at least seven of his citations were from the book of Psalms.[7]

Original composers and singers. But did the original composers and singers understand what we can with the benefit of New Testament hindsight? Did they see the Messiah in the Psalms to the extent that the New Testament writers did? These questions get to three of the core messages of this book. (See especially the exposition of 1 Peter 1:10–12 in chapter 4.)

- No Old Testament believer enjoyed the extraordinary light that New Testament believers have since Jesus died and was resurrected, and the Holy Spirit was poured out at pentecost.
- Every Old Testament believer had sufficient light to trust in a future Messiah who would suffer, die, and be glorified.
- Every Old Testament writer knew that his messages of salvation by grace through faith in the Messiah would be much clearer to future generations.

That's the way to approach the Psalms. Yes, we know much more than the original writers and singers. However, they also were looking forward to a future Messiah who would suffer a while before being glorified. And they knew that this message of salvation by grace would be much better understood when the events predicted actually took place.

In some ways, we are in a similar position to these first psalm singers when we think ahead to the *second* coming of Jesus. Many passages in the Old and New Testaments—including the Psalms—predict Jesus' coming again in great glory to end this world and create a new environment for a renewed people. But while we get the overall outline of what lies ahead, only when these events unfold in detail will we fully understand these scriptures. In the meantime, we look ahead with optimistic faith and sing psalms such as Psalm 72 and 98 with the same inquiring faith that the Old Testament prophets also experienced with reference to the first coming of Jesus.[8]

Original background. The Psalms were not composed in a vacuum. They did not appear out of nowhere, disconnected from previous history. They were written and sung by people steeped in Old Testament theology. Let me suggest several truths that saturate the book of Psalms:

- God saves by grace, not works.
- God will send a Deliverer.
- The Deliverer will reveal God in an unprecedented way.
- The Deliverer will suffer as a sacrifice for sin.
- The Deliverer will reign everywhere and forever.

That sounds very Christian, doesn't it? That's because it is.

Consider the alternative. If the Old Testament psalm singers believed they were saved by works, their salvation rested in an earthly king, and the nation of Israel would eventually reign over the world, despite some suffering along the way, then we're talking about two different, two opposite, religions. And unless we are postmodernists who could care less about the original authors' intentions and meaning, let's throw our Psalters in the sea and use only gospel choruses instead.

Oh, that's already happened, has it? That's because of a fundamental misunderstanding of Old Testament theology and psalmody, especially a denial of these fundamental pillars of Old Testament theology.

Why not go through the Old Testament looking for these pillars?

Don't worry. You'll find them quite easily. And then go back to the Psalms. Do they sound or feel different from what you've just read? Do you find believers who trust in a God who saves by grace, not works? Do you find divine promises and believers' hopes of a future extraordinary Deliverer? Do you find a love for divine revelation and a longing for more of it? Do you find prophecies and pictures of sacrificial suffering, of bloodshed and death? Do you find promises of ultimate worldwide victory for this Deliverer and everyone from every nation that puts his trust in Him? In other words, do you find Christianity? Of course you do. It's in shadow and seed form, but shadow implies some light, and seed implies continuity with the fruit.

And we find not only Christian doctrine but also Christian experience. We find believers wrestling with doubt and triumphing in faith. We find believers quaking with fear and finding refuge under the shadow of heavenly wings. We find believers being persecuted and anticipating God's future rout of their and His enemies. We find some believers anxious about dying and others ecstatic with heavenly hope. We find hearts dissatisfied with human words, feasting on divine promises. We find concern for family and nation but also unblinkered and unfettered interest in the worldwide expansion of the gospel. We find pastoral words addressed to the young and the old, to fathers and mothers, to rich and poor, to ruler and ruled. We find weakness in the flesh and longings for more of the Holy Spirit. We find mourning over the state of the church and confidence in its future triumph. What Christian experience is not covered by the Psalms? John Calvin said, "There is not an emotion of which anyone can be conscious that is not here represented as in a mirror. Or rather, the Holy Spirit has here drawn to life all the griefs, sorrows, fears, doubts, hopes, cares, perplexities, in short, all the distracting emotions with which the minds of men are wont to be agitated."[9]

And just in case you are not persuaded, have a look at Psalm 16. Read that psalm in a vacuum, without any Old Testament context or New Testament commentary. What is it all about? The psalmist addressed "LORD" and "God" a few times. It seems as if he was a theist, a Unitarian at least. He believed in God and that God was involved in his life—he was not an atheist or a deist at any rate. It also appears that he had an appreciation of grace. Although at points he seemed to boast a little about his separation from idolatry and his own steadfastness, he also looked to God as his Deliverer both in this life and in the life to come. Seems to confirm what most people think about Old Testament believers, doesn't it? They had a vague, general faith in God and sometimes mixed in their own efforts with God's grace.

But is that really a fair representation of David's faith? Thankfully the New Testament provides commentary on this passage. In Acts 2, Peter was inspired by the Holy Spirit to preach Christ as the fulfillment of Old Testament prophecy. After referencing Joel 2, he introduced Psalm 16 with these words: "David says concerning Him . . ."[10] And he concluded his quotation by explaining that David "being a prophet, and knowing that God had sworn with an oath to him that of the fruit of his body, according to the flesh, He would raise up the Christ to sit on his throne, he, foreseeing this, spoke concerning the resurrection of the Christ, that His soul was not left in Hades [Hell], nor did His flesh see corruption."[11]

Peter was not saying that although Psalm 16 shows David describing himself as a bit of a confused theist, we, as believing Christians, can read and sing that psalm of Christ. No! He was saying that David himself knew that he was not speaking about himself, that David knew he was speaking of Christ, and that David knew he was speaking of the resurrection of Christ. In other words, David, like us, was a believing Christian speaking of Christ as his only hope. Notice again how all of the pillars of Old Testament theology are found in this psalm.

But you may ask, "Was David not at times speaking of himself? His life seems to fit so many of the psalms, after all." Yes, there is no question that God in His providence arranged David's life so that he experienced many things the future messianic King would also experience, though in a much greater way. Thus God inspired David to write songs about David's own experience insofar as it mirrored and predicted the future Messiah.

There were also times when the psalmist wrote of a person and events that far transcended anything that any historical king experienced.[12] And he knew it. For example, when David called the Messiah "Lord" in Psalm 110, Jesus said that he did so intentionally, not ignorantly.[13] Calvin commented:

> In this psalm David sets forth the perpetuity of Christ's reign, and the eternity of his priesthood. . . . Having the testimony of Christ that this psalm was penned in reference to himself, we need not apply to any other quarter for the corroboration of this statement . . . the truths here stated relate neither to David nor to any other person than the Mediator alone.[14]

It's also fair to say although some psalms begin with a historical situation in David's life, they eventually escalate way above a possible historical interpretation.[15]

In summary, then, Jesus is in the Psalms, but He is in them in different ways.

WE SING WITH JESUS IN THE PSALMS

As we have seen, the book of Psalms covers every Christian experience. But the Psalms also cover every experience of Jesus. The book of Psalms was His hymnbook during His earthly life. And how suitable they were for His many spiritual needs. Christopher Wright says, "Jesus came to a people who knew how to pray, and to sing. The rich heritage of worship in Israel was part of the very fabric and furniture of the mind of Jesus. So it is not at all surprising to find him often quoting from the Psalms, even with his dying breath."[16]

As we mature in faith, psalms appropriate to our spiritual condition come naturally to us. There are explicit examples in the New Testament of this also being Jesus' experience.[17] But this was indicative of a common and constant experience in His soul. The Psalms, therefore, give us an accurate and intimate insight into the soul of Jesus. The Gospels focus largely on His outward public life, but the Psalms give us His secret inner life. When people write biographies, they often try to guess the thoughts of the subject, but here we do not need to guess. God so ordered the psalmists' lives, and so inspired their reflections, that they anticipated Jesus' thoughts and feelings. Geerhardus Vos pointed out that "our Lord himself found his inner life portrayed in the Psalter and in some of the highest moments of his ministry borrowed from it the language in which his soul spoke to God, thus recognizing that a more perfect language for communion with God cannot be framed."[18]

We may worship Jesus in the Psalms by meditating on when and how He sang them. How we wish we could have heard Him praise His heavenly Father with psalms of praise.[19] How mournfully He sang the psalms of lament as He saw the impact of sin on Himself, the church, and the community.[20] How anxiously He sang the psalms of suffering as He anticipated the sacrificial pains that lay ahead for Him.[21] How joyfully He sang the psalms of thanksgiving for the many deliverances He experienced.[22] How boldly He sang the psalms of confidence as He entrusted Himself to His heavenly Father.[23] How gladly He sang the psalms of remembrance as He recalled God's great acts in the past.[24] How soberly He sang the psalms of suffering.[25] How powerfully He sang the royal psalms.[26] How holily He sang the imprecatory psalms when He saw the spiritual devastation His enemies were causing.[27]

Just as certain psalms seem to especially fit certain seasons of our lives, so the Psalms fitted the many stages of Jesus' life: when He was a young boy, when He was a teenager, when He went to the synagogue, when He was carrying out His morning devotions, when He read the Scriptures, when He reflected on His preaching, when He defeated temptation, when He woke, when He slept, when He watched the Devil at work, when He saw souls saved, when He heard of the deaths of His followers, when He celebrated the Passover with His unique and unparalleled understanding, when the cross loomed, when He was falsely accused, when He was betrayed, when He was forsaken, and when He was dying, then rising again.[28]

What insight the book of Psalms gives us into Jesus' spiritual life! What a privilege that we can sing Jesus' hymns from His own hymnbook! As His body, we can sing the Psalms with Jesus, our Head. He is our Song Leader. Pastor Michael Lefebvre, who wrote a book on the Psalms, put it like this:

> Many modern hymns are written to Jesus, or are written about Jesus. The Psalms also include portions addressed to Christ and many lines about him. But in all the Psalms (and only in the Psalms) we have words of Christ to sing with him. Finding Jesus in the Psalms is not simply about the prophecies of his work in

this line or in that line. We find Jesus in the Psalms by hearing his voice leading our praise in every line. . . . Historically, the Psalms were treasured by the Church because they are the hymns of Jesus. The time has come for us to recover a passion for singing, not just about Jesus—but singing with him.[29]

JESUS IN THE SONG OF SOLOMON

I've left the Song of Solomon to the end, partly because its interpretation has caused so much controversy in the church and partly because much of the controversy is caused by taking the Song out of its Old Testament context. If you are still reading, I hope that by now you will have been persuaded of the Christ-centered focus of the Old Testament. Read in that context, it should be much easier to read the Song in a Christ-centered way.

I'll admit that if I were to come across a booklet in a library containing just the Song of Solomon, I would think it belonged on the romantic fiction shelves. It's a beautiful love story. But God has placed the Song right in the middle of thirty-eight Christ-centered books, and that might just give us a clue to what it's about.

A SONG TO THE COMING KING OF LOVE

Imagine you picked up a book titled *The Coming King of Love*. There are lots of stories in it telling about how some rather unlovely and unlovable people needed such a king, longed for such a king, and even predicted such a king. From time to time the King sent special messages and visions to some of these hopeful people, which they also recorded in this book, together with the King's laws. Other chapters detail certain rituals and festivals that kept the hope alive and further defined it. There are also some beautiful songs for the people to sing as they wait for the King's coming. And then in the middle of the book you find a poem that celebrates the love of the King for an undeserving woman. It's a beautiful literary tale of romantic and even passionate love.

What's your reaction?

Do you think, *This seems out of place,* or *This must be some marriage guidance for me?*

Of course not. Why would the King write a whole book about Himself and then throw in a chapter that had nothing to do with Him? As Jesus Himself said, He is to be found in *all* the Scriptures.[30]

I'm afraid so many simply consider the Song of Solomon mere marriage counseling because they do not believe that the rest of the Old Testament is about the coming King of love. And that's why I've left the Song of Solomon to the end. I want to establish that since the entire Old Testament is about Jesus, so is the Song.

That's not to imply the Song has nothing to say about human marriage. It does, but in a secondary way. That's how Paul also used the marriage between the Lord and His church, as a guide and picture of the marriage between a man and a woman.[31] And as Paul taught, it works the opposite way too.

This argument has Old Testament precedent on its side. The Old Testament covenant with Israel was pictured as a marriage, and idolatry was equated with adultery, a theme taken up by the prophets and carried into the New Testament.[32] Throughout the Bible, monogamous marriage is the norm for depicting the covenant relationship between God and His people, with it all climaxing at the marriage supper of the Lamb.[33]

So, if we are to read this book as a call to a romantic, passionate relationship with the Lord, the King of love, how do we interpret the details of the text? My answer may surprise you: we

don't. I'm afraid that many people have been turned off reading
the Song in a Christ-centered way because so many interpreters
become lost in the details.

How to Sing the Song of Songs

A few years ago, in my Old Testament exegesis class, I was
working my way through the arguments about whether the
Song was to be interpreted literally, allegorically, or typologi-
cally when I noticed one of my students smiling and shaking his
head—thankfully quite a rare occurrence. Eventually I stopped
and asked this usually courteous young man what was wrong.
He explained a little about his Middle Eastern agricultural background—probably close to the Song's original location—and
how he had studied his ancient culture's literature at a mas-
ter's level. He went on to politely express his horror at the way
we were approaching ancient Eastern literature with a modern
Western mind-set. He said that such love songs were very common in his culture and that they were to be primarily interpreted
by the emotions and impressions they evoke rather than by dis-
secting every word with dictionaries, lexicons, grammars, and so
on. These songs, he said, were primarily to provoke and stimulate
emotions rather than be subjected to cold, logical analysis.

That immediately jived with something I remembered Vern
Poythress had written on the similar disadvantage in which Western
minds find themselves when interpreting biblical typology:

> We in the West are not very much at ease with symbolism
> ourselves. We live in an industrialized society dominated by
> scientific and technological forms of knowledge. Such knowl-
> edge minimizes the play of metaphors and the personal depth

dimensions of human living. For many people "real" truth means technological truth, that is, truth swept free of metaphor and symbolism. . . . I am convinced that God does not share our general cultural aversion to metaphors and symbols. He wrote the Old Testament, which contains a good deal of poetry and many uses of metaphor. Jesus spoke in parables, which are a kind of extended metaphor. Godly Israelites of Old Testament times were able to appreciate His language, whereas we have a hard time with it. We must adapt to the fact that symbols and metaphors can speak truly and powerfully without speaking with pedantic scientific precision. . . . To appreciate a symbol, we must let our imaginations play a little, and ask what the symbol suggests. What does it bring to mind? What is it like? . . . We must explore all these questions, but endeavor to do so like an Israelite, not like a [twenty-first]-century Westerner.[34]

Though speaking about two different kinds of biblical literature, my student and Poythress were really making the same point: if we are ever going to understand the original message of the Song, we have to make a difficult journey across cultures and centuries and be more imaginative and impressionistic than scientific—and who is to say which approach is morally superior? It all depends on the divine intention.

STOP DISSECTING AND START FEELING

With the Song in particular, we have to dial down the Western academic analysis—and also the Western obsession with sex—and aim to stir up Eastern emotions and moods. Instead of parsing every word, every tree, every flower, and every body part under a microscope, we should take a step back, sing a few verses, and ask:

What impression is this intended to make upon me? What emotion does this evoke? What feeling is this calling me to experience or enjoy? And as this is a Christ-centered song, especially ask, what emotion is it calling me to feel toward Jesus? And what is it saying about Jesus' feelings toward me?

This is not easy or comfortable for most analytical Westerners who have been taught to suppress emotions and suspect impressions. It certainly doesn't come easily to me. Despite my writing a thirty-four-verse poem on a large Valentine's card when we were engaged more than twenty years ago, my wife will tell you that love poetry is not one of my strengths. Although that puts me at a significant disadvantage when it comes to interpreting Eastern love poems such as the Song of Solomon, following are some of the emotions evoked in me and impressions made upon me as I tried to read the Song as it was intended to be read—or sung. To keep it simple, I've restricted myself to the one word that sprang to mind as I felt the text:

- *Passion*: The relationship is not cold but warm and affectionate. (Song 1:2)
- *Desire*: Each longs for the other with unembarrassed anticipation and expectation. (1:2, 4; 2:10)
- *Sensory*: All the senses are stimulated—taste, smell, touch, sight, and hearing.
- *Joy*: Superabounding happiness is experienced when together. (1:4)
- *Grace*: There is amazing grace in the King's loving one so unlovely. (1:5–6)
- *Imaginative*: Much creative thought is put into expressing and articulating this love. (1:9)

- *Generosity*: Giving is more prominent than getting. (1:11)
- *Admiration*: Lots of expressions of appreciation. "O my love" occurs nine times in the book, and "my beloved" twenty-four times. (1:15–16)
- *Public*: This is not a shameful, furtive, secret love but an unashamed, unafraid, public love. (2:4)
- *Intimacy*: There is closeness, not distance; familiarity, not aloofness. (2:6; 4:5; 7:3)
- *Threats*: There are significant threats to the relationship. (2:15)
- *Change*: The relationship has its ups and downs, its peaks and troughs. (3:1; 5:6)
- *Mutuality*: This is not one-sided but two-sided. He initiates and she responds; then she initiates and he responds.
- *Beauty*: Her stunning beauty is described at length in chapter 4 and his in chapter 5.
- *Innocence*: He describes her repeatedly as a dove, a bird renowned for its loyal purity. (4:1)
- *Radiance*: Her perfect shining smile is described in unforgettably graphic terms. (4:2)
- *Health*: They are in the prime of life: healthy, vigorous, energetic, and full of color. (4:3)
- *Dignity*: Her deportment, bearing, posture, and jewelry are elegant and dignified. (4:4)
- *Discretion*: The descriptions of intimacy stop at an appropriate point: the rest is private. (4:5)
- *Excitement*: They are excited by and captivated with each other. The briefest look thrills and enraptures. (4:9)

- *Overwhelming*: Sometimes the love is too much to take in. (6:5)
- *Unique*: This love is like no other; it is incomparable. (6:8–9)
- *Fruitful*: Pregnancy is described in agricultural terms usually associated with fertility. (7:2)
- *Dependence*: She needs him and leans upon him. (8:5)
- *Jealous*: Their passionate love will not tolerate alternatives or opposition. (8:6)
- *Durable*: Their love lasts and outlasts all the tests of time. (8:7)
- *Priceless*: Money cannot buy you this kind of love. (8:7)

More sensitive hearts and more poetic minds could produce a much longer and richer list. But I hope you can begin to see the difference between this approach and the allegorical approach that tries to find a deeper spiritual meaning in every apple, nut, flower, lip, and breast.

Why not go through the list, or read the book and make your own list, and seek more of the reality of this marriage to the King of love in your life? Don't get lost in the details. What words spring to your mind, or what feelings leap out of your heart? Do they reflect your relationship with the King of love or call you into a deeper and closer experience of it? Yes, there's much here for our own marriages, but there's much more for our spiritual and eternal marriage.

I try to follow a four-step process when studying the Song:

1. Message of the Song: What's the main point, principle, impression, or feeling?

2. Message for marriage: What does that teach for marriage?
3. Message for Israel: What was this to teach Israel about its relationship to the Lord?
4. Message for New Testament church or believer: What does this teach the church or the individual believer about their, his, or her relationship to the Lord?

Let's conclude with a few examples of how to apply this impressionistic approach to particular chapters. Remember we are resisting the temptation of trying to find an exact spiritual parallel or marriage parallel for every poetic detail.

He Is Everything to Me (1:1–17)

He is beautiful, but I am damaged.
He is generous in praise and gifts.
He refreshes me.
He returns my love.
He enriches my life.

A Taste of Heaven on Earth (2:1–17)

Love is beautiful/fragrant.
Love nourishes.
Love is patient and sensitive.
Love is enthusiastic.
Love invites.
Love is bashful.
Love is tender.
Love is possessive.
Love is imperfect on earth.

He Is All-Over Lovely (5:10–16)

He is outstanding.

He is noble and royal.

He is tender.

He is fragrant.

He is rich.

He is strong and solid.

He is authoritative.

He is affectionate.

Love Wins (8:5–14)

Love returns to its roots.

Love reflects on its strengths.

Love relies on the protection and support of close friends.

Love reprioritizes relationships.

Love recognizes that it has not yet won.

Conclusion

The original readers of the Song of Solomon viewed the author as the "ultimate expression of David's royal seed . . . the Davidic King, with all the messianic connotations that status carries."[35] When they read the book or sang the Song, they saw more than the best human king's best human love. They entered into God's gracious love expressed through His anointed King to His undeserving people. Despite all their failures and faults, the Song assured them that, through the Messiah, love wins.

POSTSCRIPT

The Journey Continues

I've not arrived. I don't expect to arrive soon. In some ways I don't want to arrive.

I started out on the Emmaus road with a freshly warmed heart, and I've had numerous episodes of blessed spiritual heartburn along the way. One thing's for sure: the farther I've walked, the more I've realized how much more there is yet to explore and experience of Jesus in all the Scriptures. And I say that not with a sense of disappointment but with hope-filled expectation and excitement. Indeed, sometimes fellowship with Jesus on the Emmaus road is so deep, so happy, so satisfying that I don't want to get to the end of it.

But that's shortsighted because the Emmaus road leads eventually to face-to-face fellowship with Jesus, a fellowship that will never be interrupted by His vanishing out of our sight, not even for a second. Then spiritual heartburn will not be a mere past-tense memory or a future-tense hope, but a constant present-tense reality.

Thank you for sharing in my journey. I hope these pages have started you off on your own Emmaus road or perhaps helped you explore a new branch of it in the company of the heavenly Heart-Warmer.

There's still so much to learn. I hope you will continue the journey with me at my blog (HeadHeartHand.org/blog), where I hope to expand upon each of these introductory chapters as well as share others' blessed experiences of Jesus on every page. Click on over and join in the conversation.

STUDY QUESTIONS

CHAPTER 1: WHERE DID THE OLD TESTAMENT GO?

1. Write down some words that come into your mind when you think of the Old Testament. After you've read this book, write down a new list of words in the light of what you've learned, and compare the lists.
2. Which of the reasons for so little Old Testament teaching do you recognize? Can you think of any more?
3. When you speak of your Savior, do you use His personal name *Jesus* or His official title *Christ* more? If you use *Christ* more, what might that indicate about your spiritual life, and how will you try to change it?
4. What will you do to increase the ratio of Old Testament study in your life, in your family, and in your church?

CHAPTER 2: WHAT'S THE OLD TESTAMENT ALL ABOUT?

1. What do you think the Old Testament is all about?

2. How would you tell your story about the role of the Old Testament in your spiritual journey?

3. What's hindered your study of the Old Testament? What's helped?

4. What gospel keys have you found? Has any one book or sermon been of particular help to you?

CHAPTER 3: JESUS' ANSWER

1. What are the advantages of reading the Old Testament with the help of the New Testament? Can you think of any disadvantages?

2. Can you think of any other situations where knowing the ultimate goal or destination helped you understand everything else?

3. Which Old Testament passages or sermons have given you blessed spiritual heartburn?

4. When you read about Abraham's life in Genesis, can you find events that might have helped him to see Jesus' day with joy?

5. Where does Moses write about Jesus?[1]

6. How is it possible for people to read the Scriptures in pursuit of eternal life and yet not find it?[2]

CHAPTER 4: PETER'S ANSWER

1. Where do we see evidence that the Holy Spirit was in the Old Testament prophets?

2. Provide examples of where the Old Testament prophets predict (a) Jesus' sufferings and (b) Jesus' glory.

3. Discuss or think about Wayne Grudem's idea of "acted-out prophecies" in the lives of Old Testament characters. How does this change the way you read the Old Testament?

4. How much do you think the prophets knew about what they were saying and writing? What help did the prophets have in understanding what they said and wrote?[3]

5. Can you think of any life experiences where you really understood something only when you experienced it rather than just studied it?

6. What does Psalm 22 tell you about Jesus on the cross that you cannot find out from the Gospels?

7. What were the similarities between the Old Testament prophets and the New Testament apostles?

Chapter 5: Paul's Answer

1. How was a person saved in the Old Testament?

2. Read Romans 1–11, and make a note of the passages proving that Paul viewed Old Testament religion the same as the New Testament's religion.

3. Reread Galatians 3–4 from the perspective you've gained from reading this chapter. What difference does it make?

4. Try to remember the bondage you experienced before Jesus set you free by His grace. Why do you think the Galatians and many Christians find it so hard to rest in the freedom that Jesus gives?

5. Exodus 19:1–6 shows God's pattern of Redemption, then Relationship, then Rules. Why is this order important? How does the pattern help you better live the Christian life?

6. In what ways is the gospel of Jesus the same as the gospel of Moses? In what ways is it different?

7. Having read this chapter, how would you now describe the way of salvation in the Old Testament?

CHAPTER 6: JOHN'S ANSWER

1. Can you think of other ways to illustrate the difference between an absolute contrast and a relative contrast?

2. The writer of Hebrews stated, "For indeed the gospel was preached to us as well as to them."[4] Who was the apostle writing about? In what ways was the gospel preached to them?

3. Quote examples of God's giving grace in the Old Testament.

4. Have you confessed that like the disciples you have been foolish and "slow of heart to believe in all that the prophets have spoken"?[5]

CHAPTER 7: CHRIST'S PLANET: DISCOVERING JESUS IN THE CREATION

1. Before you read this chapter, what did you think Genesis 1–2 was all about?

2. This chapter focuses on how the creation was created *by* Christ. In what ways was it created *for* Him?[6]

3. We saw how reading Genesis 1–2 through the eyes of the original readers, the Israelites, helps us understand why these words were written. Try to do the same with other

narratives in Genesis, then in Exodus, and other books. How does it change the way you understand these scriptures?

4. In what way is creation a redemptive event?

5. How does understanding the original creation of the world help us understand the purpose of salvation, often presented as a new creation?[7]

6. What other creatures and objects did Jesus make to teach us about Himself and His salvation?

7. In what ways do angels serve you as an heir of salvation?[8]

8. Consider the order of creation and describe how it parallels the advance of salvation in your soul.

9. Explain how you experience salvation as (a) a Sabbath and (b) a marriage.

10. What does the Lord reveal about Himself through His creation?[9]

11. In what ways do you show that you've been created by Jesus and for Jesus?

Chapter 8: Christ's People: Discovering Jesus in the Old Testament Characters

1. In what ways have you fallen into the "heroes and villains" approach to the Old Testament? What weaknesses can you see in this way of reading and teaching the Old Testament?

2. Sidney Greidanus gave a good example of how to view David's story in light of the bigger story of redemption. Pick another Old Testament narrative or biography, and try to draw lessons by using the same structure: (a) personal history, (b) national history, and (c) redemptive history.

3. How do the graces and gifts of Old Testament believers bring glory to Jesus?

4. Job's patience in suffering and Joseph's forgiveness of his persecuting brothers are the work of Christ's Spirit and reflect the formation of Christ's image in them. What other Old Testament characters and their graces show us Christ's work and image in them?

5. What new questions will you be asking when you read Old Testament books? Try it with a few books, and see what answers you get.

6. In what ways does seeing our sins as being against Jesus help us repent and turn from our sins?

7. Summarize the role of animal sacrifice in the spiritual experience of Old Testament believers.

8. Explain how Old Testament believers were saved by Jesus before Jesus was born, suffered, died, and rose again.

9. How do Old Testament believers motivate worship and imitation of Jesus?

10. What kind of life do Old Testament saints enjoy in heaven?[10] How does that help us with our lives here on earth?

Chapter 9: Christ's Presence: Discovering Jesus in His Old Testament Appearances

1. Some verses in the Bible tell us that no one can see God and live.[11] How is it then that some Old Testament believers saw God and lived (for example, Hagar, Jacob, Moses, and Manoah)? Look up John 1:18; 2 Corinthians 4:6; Colossians 1:15; and 1 Timothy 2:5.

How do these verses help us understand this seeming inconsistency?

2. How can modern believers see God and live? How does Jesus come to you today?

3. John Calvin said: "Holy men of old knew God only by beholding him in his Son as in a mirror (cf. 2 Cor. 3:18). When I say this, I mean that God has never manifested himself to men in any other way than through the Son, that is, his sole wisdom, light, and truth."[12] These are strong words. The Reformer seemed to be saying that God gave no revelation except through His Son. Can you think of supporting or contrary examples? If that Reformer was right, how would that affect our understanding of Scripture, especially the Old Testament?

4. What parallels do you notice between the Angel of the Lord's encounter with Hagar in Genesis 16 and Jesus' encounter with the woman of Samaria in John 4?

5. Many of us have probably conceived of Christ's ministry in the Old Testament as occasional or exceptional, but John Walvoord says that it was clearly "common and continual." How could this perspective change how we read the Old Testament?

6. If the Old Testament appearances of Christ indicate His longing to be with us, how does Christ communicate that to us today?

7. If the Old Testament appearances of Christ created a longing in believers for His first coming, how do we cultivate and strengthen our desire and longing for His second coming?

8. Look up these passages that also describe appearances of

the Angel of the Lord. What do we learn about the Angel's character and role in these passages?

- Numbers 22:22–38
- Judges 2:1–3
- Judges 6:11–24
- Zechariah 1:12–21
- Joshua 5:13–15

9. It is common to hear the God of the Old Testament contrasted with the God of the New Testament. In what ways does the Angel of the Lord help us see that the God of the Old Testament is the same as the God of the New Testament?

CHAPTER 10: CHRIST'S PRECEPTS: DISCOVERING JESUS IN THE OLD TESTAMENT LAW

1. Why is it important to distinguish three kinds of Old Testament law?
2. Can you think of (a) a moral law that continues today, (b) a ceremonial law that was abolished by Jesus' death, and (c) one of Israel's civil laws that give us a helpful principle of justice for our own day?
3. How does the fact that the Son of God gave the Ten Commandments to Moses change the way you view them?[13]
4. What can you learn about Jesus' character from reading His law?
5. Can you think of examples where Jesus used Old Testament law in His teaching?
6. What place does the law have in evangelism?
7. "The cross shows us not only the gospel of Jesus but also the law of Jesus." How would you explain this statement?

8. The Old Testament has many examples of divine judgment upon sin. What do they teach us about the final judgment?
9. What role does the law have in fellowshiping with Jesus?
10. How does the law lift up Jesus in your mind and heart?

CHAPTER 11: CHRIST'S PAST: DISCOVERING JESUS IN OLD TESTAMENT HISTORY

1. What are the similarities and differences between salvation in the Old Testament and salvation in the New Testament?
2. When did Christ begin to save sinners?
3. What's the connection between the first gospel promise in Genesis 3:15 and the first animal sacrifice in Genesis 4?
4. Who was the first believer to enter heaven?
5. How did Old Testament believers experience the Holy Spirit?
6. Who was the first preacher, and what was his message?
7. Describe Jesus' education.
8. What did Jesus learn from reading the Old Testament?
9. Read a passage of Scripture while imagining how Jesus read it and learned from it.
10. What are the benefits of singing Jesus' songs?
11. How does the humanity of Jesus help you as a Christian?

CHAPTER 12: CHRIST'S PROPHETS: DISCOVERING JESUS IN THE OLD TESTAMENT PROPHETS

1. What can we learn about God's ultimate and final prophet from the various Old Testament prophets?

2. Can you think of Old Testament examples of (a) a literal prophecy and (b) a symbolic prophecy? Why is this distinction important?

3. Give examples of the different kinds of prophetic fulfillment highlighted in this chapter.

4. According to the prophets, what are our mission and message to heathen nations?

5. How can the church learn from the prophecies addressed to Israel?

6. If the Old Testament prophets came to your church, what would they say?

7. If Jesus is the fulfillment of Israel, how does that change the way you read about Israel in the Old Testament?

CHAPTER 13: CHRIST'S PICTURES: DISCOVERING JESUS IN THE OLD TESTAMENT TYPES

1. When have pictures helped you understand something complicated?

2. Using the definition given at the beginning of this chapter, contrast a type with an allegory.

   An allegory has these main characteristics:

   • It is a story, an object, a person, or an event.
   • The story, object, and so on need not be true, real, or factual.
   • It has a deeper and different truth than the ordinary reading of the words would suggest.

EXAMPLE: (Allegory is extremely rare in Scripture. However, there are a few isolated examples.) In Judges 9:7–21 Jotham used an allegory about trees and bushes to teach his hearers how to view Abimelech's kingship. The story he told was not true. Trees and bushes did not talk to one another or bow down to one another. The story was about a much deeper truth than talking trees. It was about the nature of true kingship. This is a classic allegory.

3. What helped the Israelites understand typology?
4. Why was typology such a suitable vehicle for teaching the Israelites?
5. How did God use types to save Israelites?
6. What kinds of resemblances are you looking for in a type?
7. Take an Old Testament type, and show how the New Testament fulfillment enlarged, clarified, and heightened it.
8. How does the New Testament help us understand the Old Testament types?
9. How do the Old Testament types help us understand the New Testament?

Chapter 14: Christ's Promises: Discovering Jesus in the Old Testament Covenants

1. What was your view of a covenant before reading this chapter? In what way has it changed?
2. Give examples from ordinary life of how we use *new* to mean both "brand-new" and "renewed."
3. What forms the background of every covenant God made in the Bible? How does that encourage you in your relationship with the Lord?
4. When has God taken the initiative in your faith journey?

5. How does an understanding of the Old Testament covenants help you better profit from the Lord's Supper?

6. Try to recall the one word that sums up each of the divine covenants, together with the accompanying signs.

7. Who benefited from the Old Testament covenants, and how? What does that teach you about benefiting from the new covenant sacraments of the Lord's Supper and baptism?

8. How would you sum up the essence of the biblical covenants?

9. What's new about the new covenant, and in what way does that affect your spiritual life?

CHAPTER 15: CHRIST'S PROVERBS: DISCOVERING JESUS IN THE OLD TESTAMENT PROVERBS

1. Read Proverbs 11, and trace each proverb to one of the Ten Commandments. What does that tell you about Proverbs?

2. Read Proverbs 12, and think about how each proverb describes the life and character of Jesus.

3. In what ways do you demonstrate the clarity of the choice between wisdom and folly in your parenting and in your witness outside the home?

4. Describe how Proverbs shows you your spiritual need and the sufficiency and suitability of Jesus as Savior.

5. Can you find any area of life not covered by Proverbs? Read through some chapters and list verses that guide us in our use of social media like Facebook.

6. How does Proverbs 8 change the way you read Genesis 1?

7. Consider some parallels and contrasts between Solomon and Jesus.

8. In what ways does Wisdom's "evangelism" in Proverbs 1–9 influence the way you evangelize?

9. Read through Proverbs, asking Jesus to show you your folly and His wisdom. List ways in which He does this.

CHAPTER 16: CHRIST'S POETS: DISCOVERING JESUS IN THE OLD TESTAMENT POEMS

1. Pick a few of the Psalms, and sing them with trinitarian tongues. Think especially of Jesus when you sing them.

2. What are three of the core messages of *Jesus on Every Page*?

3. In what way is our spiritual experience awaiting the second coming of Jesus the same as that of the Old Testament believers who were awaiting His first coming?

4. What five truths saturate the Psalms?

5. What Christian experiences do you find in the Psalms?

6. I recently heard a preacher say, "The Old Testament believers had no idea of the Trinity." How would you disprove that from Psalm 16 and Psalm 110?

7. In what ways can we say that Jesus is in the Psalms?

8. In what ways can we sing with Jesus in the Psalms? Pick a psalm, and imagine Jesus singing it during His earthly life.

9. What's the key to seeing the Song of Solomon as a Christ-centered book?

10. What skills and abilities do you need to develop to read the Song of Solomon with spiritual profit?

11. Pick a chapter from the Song of Solomon, and write down the impressions and feelings evoked.

Postscript: The Journey Continues

1. What have you learned about the Bible from this book?
2. What have you learned about Jesus from this book?
3. What have you learned about yourself from this book?
4. What are you going to change in your life and ministry as a result of reading this book?

ACKNOWLEDGMENTS

Iowe so much debt to so many people in my life; I feel that printed words of thanks are just very loose change in comparison. However, as printed words are all I have in this forum, let me begin by thanking my beloved parents. Thank you, Dad and Mom, for showing me Jesus Christ, especially for showing me His love, compassion, patience, and forgiveness during my years of foolish rebellion.

Thank you to the Reverend Angus Smith, my father-in-law, who has preached Jesus now for almost sixty years. Thank you, Angus, for exemplifying the best in Scottish Highland preaching of Christ from the Old Testament.

I'm also deeply indebted to Drs. Joel Beeke and Jerry Bilkes for inviting me to join them on the faculty of Puritan Reformed Seminary. This book took a quantum leap forward when you asked me to deliver a series of lectures, "Preaching Christ from the Old Testament," at the seminary. I am especially thankful for the opportunity to spread my passion for preaching Jesus from the Old Testament throughout the world, through our amazing international student body. And thank you, Joel, for ministering to my soul so often with your Christ-centered preaching through the book of Genesis.

I have leaned heavily on some wonderful books already written, as will be obvious from the references. Thank you to these authors for their manifold labors. I hope I have managed to give all the credit where credit is due.

When I started writing this book, I had in view a book for preachers and seminary students. However, thanks to the influence and guidance of Nancy Guthrie, I eventually bit the bullet and followed the harder path of writing something for the wider Christian public. Through her prompting, I've labored to simplify and summarize so that the book's usefulness will be maximized. The more academic material has been left on the cutting room floor, along with much of my sweat and tears.

I also have Nancy to thank for putting me in touch with Legacy Management and D. J. Snell. He and Crosland Stuart have been encouraging and inspirational agents in every way.

I'm deeply grateful to Joel Miller at Thomas Nelson for his faith in this project and for his great team of editors and designers, including Janene MacIvor, Dimples Kellogg, and Lori Lynch.

Capital letter THANKS to my darling wife, Shona. Shona, God has fitted you so perfectly to my needs and ministry. Thank you for sharing my passion for this subject and for all the hours you have sacrificed to see the book through to this point.

And last but not least, thanks to the God of all grace. I cannot but daily utter with grateful and adoring astonishment the words of the apostle Paul:

To me, who am less than the least of all the saints, this grace was given, that I should preach among the Gentiles the unsearchable riches of Christ, and to make all see what is the fellowship of the mystery, which from the beginning of the ages has been hidden in God who created all things through Jesus Christ; to the intent that now the manifold wisdom of God might be made known by the church to the principalities and powers in the heavenly places, according to the eternal purpose which He accomplished in Christ Jesus our Lord, in whom we have boldness and access with confidence through faith in Him.[1]

NOTES

PREFACE
1. Luke 24:25.
2. Luke 24:32.

CHAPTER 1: WHERE DID THE OLD TESTAMENT GO?
1. Gleason L. Archer, "A New Look at the Old Testament," *Decision*, August 1972, 5.

CHAPTER 3: JESUS' ANSWER
1. Luke 24:25–26.
2. Graeme Goldsworthy, *According to Plan* (Downers Grove, IL: IVP, 1991), 55.
3. Luke 24:26–27, 44.
4. Matthew 5:17–18.
5. John 8:56.
6. Galatians 3:8, emphasis added.
7. Genesis 3:15.
8. Hebrews 11:8–9.
9. Luke 1:54–55, 72–73.
10. Genesis 15:6.
11. John 5:39, 46.

CHAPTER 4: PETER'S ANSWER
1. 1 Peter 1:11.
2. Wayne Grudem, *Commentary on 1 Peter* (Leicester: IVP, 1995), 69.
3. 1 Peter 1:10–11.
4. Grudem, *Commentary on 1 Peter*, 70.

5. 1 Peter 1:10.
6. 1 Peter 1:11.
7. J. Ramsey Michaels, *Word Biblical Commentary* vol. 49, *1 Peter,* (Dallas: Word, Incorporated, 1998), 44.
8. Walter C. Kaiser, *The Uses of the Old Testament in the New* (Chicago: Moody, 1985), 20.
9. 1 Peter 1:12.
10. Sidney Greidanus, *Preaching Christ from the Old Testament* (Grand Rapids: Eerdmans, 1999), 136.
11. Luke 24:49; Acts 1:8; 2:33.

CHAPTER 5: PAUL'S ANSWER

1. Philippians 3:5.
2. Galatians 4:21.
3. Galatians 4:22.
4. Galatians 4:22–23.
5. Galatians 4:24 KJV.
6. Galatians 4:24.
7. Ibid.
8. Exodus 12:24–25.
9. Exodus 20:2–26.
10. Christopher Wright, "Preaching from the Law," in *Reclaiming the Old Testament for Christian Preaching*, Grenville J. R. Kent, Paul J. Kissling, and Laurence A. Turner, eds. (Downers Grove, IL: IVP, 2010), 48.
11. Galatians 3:17, 19, 21.
12. Galatians 3:6–9.
13. Galatians 3:17.
14. Galatians 3:15.
15. Galatians 3:21.
16. Galatians 3:19.
17. Galatians 3:24.
18. Galatians 3:25–26.
19. Exodus 19:4; 20:1–2.
20. Exodus 19:5; 20:3–4.
21. Exodus 19:5.
22. Wright, "Preaching from the Law," 49.
23. Luke 16:29–31.
24. Hebrews 11:24, 27–29.
25. Hebrews 11:26.
26. Galatians 4:25.
27. Galatians 4:30–31.
28. 2 Corinthians 3:6, 7, 9.
29. 2 Corinthians 3:6, 8–9.

30. Victor A. Shepherd, *The Nature and Function of Faith in the Theology of John Calvin* (Macon, GA: Mercer University Press, 1983), 144, citing Augustine.
31. 2 Corinthians 3:7, 11–12.
32. 2 Corinthians 3:12 KJV.
33. 2 Corinthians 3:14.
34. Charles Hodge, *2 Corinthians* (London: James Nisbet, 1877), 70–71, 73.

CHAPTER 6: JOHN'S ANSWER

1. John 1:17.
2. 2 Corinthians 3:11.
3. Rodney Whitacre, *Commentary on John* (Downers Grove, IL: IVP, 1999), 60–61.
4. Ibid., 60–61.
5. Matthew Henry, *Matthew Henry's Commentary on the Whole Bible: Complete and Unabridged in One Volume* (Peabody: Hendrickson, 1994), John 1:15–18.
6. Hebrews 4:2, emphasis added.
7. E.g., John 3:14; 5:46; 6:32.
8. John 1:9, emphasis added.
9. John 1:15.
10. John 1:16.
11. Luke 24:32.

CHAPTER 7: CHRIST'S PLANET: DISCOVERING JESUS IN THE CREATION

1. Colossians 1:16, emphasis added.
2. Ephesians 1:4.
3. Revelation 13:8, emphasis added.
4. 1 Peter 1:20, emphasis added.
5. Jonathan Edwards, *The Works of Jonathan Edwards*, vol. 1, *A History of the Work of Redemption* (Peabody: MA: Hendrickson, 2004), 534.
6. Genesis 1:27.
7. 2 Corinthians 4:4; Colossians 1:15.
8. Colossians 3:10.
9. Revelation 1:6.
10. John 10.
11. Matthew 6:25–27.
12. Matthew 19:24.
13. Song 2:1.
14. John 4:14.
15. Hebrews 1:14.
16. Mark 1:13.

17. Luke 22:43.
18. 2 Corinthians 5:17.
19. Genesis 1:2; John 6:63.
20. Genesis 1:3; 2 Corinthians 4:6.
21. Genesis 1:4; 1 Thessalonians 5:5.
22. Genesis 1:11; Galatians 5:22–23.
23. Genesis 1:27; Romans 8:28–29; Colossians 3:10.
24. Genesis 1:28–31; Romans 16:20; Ephesians 1:3; Hebrews 2:6–9.
25. Romans 5:12–21; 1 Corinthians 15:22.
26. Romans 5:12–21; 1 Corinthians 15:21–22, 45–49.
27. Matthew 11:28; Hebrews 4:1–12; Revelation 14:13.
28. Ephesians 5:24–27; Revelation 19:9.
29. Matthew 25:34.
30. Colossians 1:16.
31. Mark 4:41.
32. Genesis 1:20–22, 29.
33. Genesis 1:22, 28; 2:3.

CHAPTER 8: CHRIST'S PEOPLE: DISCOVERING JESUS IN THE OLD TESTAMENT CHARACTERS

1. Haddon Robinson, *Biblical Preaching* (Grand Rapids: Baker, 2001), 94.
2. Haddon Robinson and Craig Brian Larson, *The Art and Craft of Biblical Preaching: A Comprehensive Resource for Today* (Grand Rapids: Zondervan, 2009), 23.
3. David F. Wells, "The D-Min-ization of the Ministry," in *No God but God*, Os Guinness and John Seel, eds. (Chicago: Moody, 1992), 184–85.
4. Sidney Greidanus, *The Modern Preacher and the Ancient Text* (Grand Rapids: Eerdmans, 1988), 118, emphasis in original.
5. 1 Samuel 17.
6. 1 Samuel 17:45–47.
7. Revelation 20:10. Greidanus, *Preaching Christ*, 239.
8. Romans 4:22–24.
9. Romans 15:4; 1 Corinthians 10:1, 6, 11.
10. James 5:10–11, 17.
11. Hebrews 11:1—12:2.
12. Luke 17:32.
13. John Owen, *Hebrews: The Epistle of Warning* (Grand Rapids: Kregel Publications, 1977), 49.
14. Bryan Chapell, *Christ-Centered Preaching* (Grand Rapids: Baker Academic, 2005), 276.
15. Romans 4:1–3; James 5:11.
16. 1 Peter 1:11.
17. Acts 7:38 KJV.

18. John 5:39.

19. Matthew 13:17.

20. 1 Peter 1:10–11.

21. Acts 3:21, 24, emphasis added.

22. Deuteronomy 18:15.

23. John 5:46.

24. Ernst Jenni and Claus Westermann, *Theological Lexicon of the Old Testament* (Peabody, MA: Hendrickson Publishers, 1997), 289.

25. Ruth 4:17–22.

26. Galatians 3:19 KJV; Acts 7:53.

27. Psalms 51:4.

28. Luke 4:1–13.

29. Nehemiah 13:14, 22, 29.

30. Hebrews 10:4.

31. Hebrews 10:3.

32. Psalms 51:17.

33. Hebrews 9:9, 13.

34. John Calvin, *Institutes* 2.7.1. John T. McNeill, ed. Ford Lewis Battles, trans. (Philadelphia: Westminster Press, 1960), 349.

35. Psalms 51:16–17.

36. Isaiah 53.

37. Job 9:33; 19:25.

38. Hebrews 11:31–32.

39. Hebrews 4:2; 11:26.

40. Matthew 8:11.

41. Genesis 49:10.

42. Westminster Confession of Faith, 8.6. (Pronouns capitalized.)

43. Hebrews 11:13–26; 12:2.

44. Charles D. Drew, *The Ancient Love Song* (Phillipsburg, NJ: P&R, 2000), 45.

45. Michael Rydelnik, *The Messianic Hope* (Nashville: B&H, 2010), 86.

46. Drew, *The Ancient Love Song*, 48.

47. Ibid., 46.

48. Ibid.

49. Articles of Religion, http://anglicansonline.org/basic/thirty-nine_articles.html.

50. Matthew 8:11 KJV.

51. Hebrews 12:22–23 KJV.

CHAPTER 9: CHRIST'S PRESENCE: DISCOVERING JESUS IN HIS OLD TESTAMENT APPEARANCES

1. Jonathan Edwards, *The History of Redemption* (Edinburgh: Banner of Truth, 2003); Jonathan Stephens, *Theophany: Close Encounters with the Son of God* (Epsom: Dayone, 2007).

2. John 1:3; Colossians 1:16; Hebrews 1:2.

3. Colossians 1:17; Hebrews 1:3.

4. John 1:1, 14.

5. John Calvin, *Institutes* 4.8.5, John T. McNeill, ed. Ford Lewis Battles, trans. (Philadelphia: Westminster Press, 1960), 349.

6. Revelation 19:10.

7. John 1:18; cf. Exodus 33:20; John 5:37; 1 Timothy 6:16; 1 John 4:12, 20.

8. Hebrews 11:27.

9. Edwards, *The History of Redemption*, 23.

10. Tertullian, quoted in Richard Watson, *Evidences, Doctrines, Morals and Institutions of Christianity* (New York: T. Mason and G. Lane, 1836), 1:501.

11. Hebrews 1:14.

12. Malachi 3:1; Luke 7:27, emphasis added.

13. John 14:9.

14. Hebrews 1:3.

15. Genesis 16:10; 22:15–16.

16. 2 Samuel 24:16; Zechariah 1:12.

17. Genesis 16:7–8.

18. Genesis 16:11.

19. Genesis 16:13.

20. Judges 5:23; 2 Kings 19:35; Genesis 48:15–16.

21. Exodus 23:20–21.

22. Judges 6:20–21, 24.

23. Genesis 22:12, 15–16.

24. Genesis 31:11–13.

25. Judges 13:21–22.

26. Exodus 23:21.

27. Charles Hodge, *Systematic Theology* vol. 1 (1872; repr., Oak Harbor, WA: Logos Research Systems, 1997), 485.

28. Revealing (Ex. 3), redeeming (Gen. 48:16), covenanting (Gen. 15:8–21), interceding (Zech. 12:1–13), protecting (Ps. 34:7), comforting (Gen. 16:7–13), commissioning (Judg. 6:11–23), and judging (2 Kings 19:35).

29. John F. Walvoord, *Jesus Christ Our Lord* (Chicago: Moody, 1969), 53.

30. Anthony T. Hanson, *Jesus Christ in the Old Testament* (London: SPCK, 1965), 172.

31. Charles D. Drew, *The Ancient Love Song* (Phillipsburg, NJ: P&R, 2000), 28.

32. Michael Barrett, *Beginning at Moses* (Greenville: Ambassador-Emerald International), 154–160.

33. Genesis 16:10.

34. Judges 13:19–20.

35. Genesis 19; Exodus 23:20–23.

36. Exodus 13:21; 14:19.

37. Cf. 1 Corinthians 10:4–9.

38. Exodus 24:10–11.

39. Exodus 33:9–11.
40. Exodus 33:14–15.
41. Hebrews 4:15 KJV.
42. Isaiah 63:8–9.
43. Exodus 19:16–25; 24:16–18.
44. Acts 7:38.
45. Exodus 40:34–38; John 1:14.
46. Leviticus 16:2; cf. Psalm 80:1.
47. Exodus 33:18; 34:5.
48. Matthew 17:5.
49. John 1:14, emphasis added.
50. Acts 1:11; Revelation 1:7 KJV.

CHAPTER 10: CHRIST'S PRECEPTS: DISCOVERING JESUS IN THE
OLD TESTAMENT LAW
1. Matthew 5:17.
2. Romans 2:14–15.
3. Westminster Confession of Faith, 19.5; hereafter cited as WCF.
4. John 2:19; Colossians 2:14.
5. WCF, 19.3.
6. Ibid., 19.4.
7. Christopher Wright, "Preaching from the Law," in *Reclaiming the Old Testament for Christian Preaching*, ed. Grenville J. R. Kent, Paul J. Kissling, and Laurence A. Turner, eds. (Downers Grove, IL: IVP, 2010), 48.
8. John 1:1.
9. 2 Timothy 3:16.
10. Acts 7:38.
11. Hebrews 7:26.
12. Deuteronomy 4:8.
13. Deuteronomy 4:40; 28:1–14.
14. Psalm 40:8.
15. Galatians 4:4.
16. Matthew 5:17; Philippians 2:7–8.
17. Matthew 5:21–48.
18. Luke 4:1–13.
19. 2 Corinthians 5:21.
20. Matthew 5:21–48.
21. Matthew 5:8.
22. Deuteronomy 26:12–15; Mark 12:41–44; Matthew 23:23.
23. WCF, 19.6.
24. Jeremiah 31:31–34.
25. Matthew 8:29.
26. Luke 5:8.

27. Galatians 3:24–25.
28. Galatians 3:10–13.
29. Leviticus 24:20; Obadiah 15.
30. 1 Peter 2:24, emphasis added.
31. Exodus 21:30; 30:12.
32. Matthew 20:28; 1 Peter 1:18–19.
33. Psalm 69:4.
34. Deuteronomy 13:11; 19:20.
35. Romans 6:2–3; Galatians 5:24.
36. Romans 8:3–4; cf. 2 Corinthians 3:18; 5:17.
37. Romans 8:19–22; Ephesians 1:10–12; Colossians 1:20.
38. Acts 17:31; 2 Corinthians 5:10.
39. Deuteronomy 28:1–14.
40. Leviticus 26:12.
41. Exodus 19:3–6.
42. John 14:21; cf. 2 Corinthians 3:18.
43. WCF, 19.6.
44. Wright, "Preaching from the Law," 51.
45. Isaiah 42:21.

CHAPTER 11: CHRIST'S PAST: DISCOVERING JESUS IN OLD TESTAMENT HISTORY
1. Donald G. Miller, *The Way to Biblical Preaching* (Nashville: Abingdon, 1957), 134.
2. Jonathan Edwards, *The Works of Jonathan Edwards*, vol. 9, *A History of the Work of Redemption* (New Haven and London: Yale University Press, 1989), 117–18.
3. Ibid., 129.
4. Ibid., 130.
5. Ibid., 139.
6. Ibid., 135.
7. Ibid., 139–40.
8. Genesis 4:26 KJV.
9. Edwards, *History of the Work of Redemption*, 143.
10. John 3:5; Romans 8:9.
11. John 7:35–39.
12. Genesis 5:22.
13. Jude 14–15.
14. Edwards, *History of the Work of Redemption*, 144.
15. Genesis 5:24.
16. Edwards, *History of the Work of Redemption*, 145.
17. Luke 2:40.
18. Mark 13:32.

19. Christopher J. H. Wright, *Knowing Jesus through the Old Testament* (Downers Grove, IL: IVP, 1992), ix.

20. Romans 9:3 KJV.

21. Wright, *Knowing Jesus through the Old Testament*, 108.

22. Matthew 11:3–5.

23. Messiah (Isa. 61:1–3), Commander of the Lord's army (Josh. 5:14), Counselor and Prince of Peace (Isa. 9:6), Servant (Isa. 52:13), Man of Sorrows (Isa. 53:3), Rock (Deut. 32:4), and Lamb (Isa. 53).

24. Wright, *Knowing Jesus through the Old Testament*, 44.

25. Matthew 12:5–6.

26. Mark 4:12.

27. Matthew 12:39–41.

28. Matthew 12:42.

29. Luke 20:41–44.

30. Luke 4:1–14.

31. E.g., Psalms 1; 37:11.

32. Richard T. France, *Jesus and the Old Testament* (Vancouver, BC: Regent College Publishing, 1998), 60.

33. Ibid.

34. Romans 11:15–25.

35. Wright, *Knowing Jesus through the Old Testament*, 241–42.

36. John MacArthur, *The Jesus You Can't Ignore* (Nashville: Thomas Nelson, 2008), 29.

37. B. B. Warfield, "The Human Development of Jesus," *Selected Shorter Writings*, vol. 1 (Phillipsburg: P&R, 1970), 161.

38. Ibid., 166.

CHAPTER 12: CHRIST'S PROPHETS: DISCOVERING JESUS IN THE OLD TESTAMENT PROPHETS

1. Deuteronomy 18:15–19; Acts 3:20–22.

2. Exodus 19:18–21.

3. Deuteronomy 18:15–19.

4. John 6:14; 7:40.

5. E.g., Deuteronomy 18:15; Amos 7:14–15.

6. Deuteronomy 18:18.

7. John 12:49; 14:10.

8. E.g., Isaiah 52:11; 2 Corinthians 6:17; Revelation 18:4.

9. E.g., Daniel 7–12; Ezekiel 33–48.

10. John 2:21; 7:38–39.

11. Numbers 24:17–20.

12. Matthew 2:1–10.

13. Revelation 22:16.

14. Walter C. Kaiser, *The Uses of the Old Testament in the New* (Chicago:

Moody, 1985), 3.

15. Sidney Greidanus, *Preaching Christ from the Old Testament* (Grand Rapids: Eerdmans, 1999), 207, quoting Christopher J. H. Wright, *Knowing Jesus through the Old Testament* (Downers Grove, IL: IVP, 1992), 63.

16. E.g., Isaiah 41:9; 42:1; 53:11.

17. Matthew 21:13; fulfillment of Isaiah 56:7 and Jeremiah 7:11.

18. Matthew 2:23; John 7:38; Ephesians 5:14; James 4:5.

19. Kaiser, *The Uses of the Old Testament in the New*, 4.

20. E.g., Isaiah 53; Psalm 22.

21. Matthew 2:23.

22. Matthew 2:5–6.

23. Isaiah 42:6; 49:22.

24. Ezekiel 42:15–19.

25. Great blessing (Isa. 61:1); great judgment ("the day of vengeance of our God" [Isa. 61:2]).

26. Luke 4:17–19.

27. Isaiah 1:27; 29:22; 35:9; 41:14; 43:16–21; 44:6, 22–24; 47:4; 48:17, 20; 49:7, 26; 51:10.

28. E.g., Genesis 3:15.

29. Christopher J. H. Wright, *Knowing Jesus through the Old Testament* (Downers Grove, IL: IVP, 1992), 71.

30. Joel 2:28.

31. Wright, *Knowing Jesus through the Old Testament*, 77.

32. E.g., Acts 3:18–24; 4:8–12; 7:52; 8:34–35; 13:23, 27, 33–37; 17:1–3, 10–15; 26:22–23; 28:23.

33. E.g., Isaiah 13–24; Ezekiel 25–32; Nahum.

34. Genesis 3:15.

35. Daniel 11:31.

36. Revelation 18:10; 11:8; 20:8.

37. Matthew 25:32–34; Luke 21:25.

38. Colossians 2:15.

39. Isaiah 16:5; 17:6–7; 18:7; 19:16–25.

40. E.g., Isaiah 60:3, 5.

41. Matthew 24:14; 28:19.

42. Matthew 4:15; 12:21.

43. Matthew 28:19.

44. Romans 9–11.

45. Acts 7:38; Hebrews 8:8, 10; 12:22; Revelation 21:2, 10.

46. Proverbs 3:12.

47. Hosea 11:1; Matthew 2:15.

48. O. P. Robertson, *The Christ of the Prophets* (Phillispburg: P&R, 2004), 6–7.

49. Matthew 4:17.

50. Ezekiel 30:3; Joel 1:15; Obadiah 15; Zephaniah 1:7, 14.
51. Isaiah 13:6; Joel 2:31–32; Zechariah 14:1.
52. Matthew 24:21; 2 Peter 3:10–12; Revelation 9:6–9.
53. Acts 26:22–23.
54. John 1:45.

CHAPTER 13: CHRIST'S PICTURES: DISCOVERING JESUS IN THE OLD TESTAMENT TYPES

1. Romans 5:19.
2. Galatians 4:25–26; Hebrews 12:22; Revelation 21:2.
3. John 1:14; Hebrews 9:8–9; Revelation 21:3.
4. Genesis 6–8; Matthew 24:37–39.
5. Acts 3:22; Hebrews 3:1; Revelation 7:15.
6. Hebrews 5:10–14.
7. Patrick Fairbairn, *The Typology of Scripture* (Grand Rapids: Kregel, 1989), 21–23.
8. Hebrews 10:1.
9. John 20:30; 21:25.
10. John 12:16.
11. Fairbairn, *Typology of Scripture*, 112.
12. Ibid.
13. Vern Poythress, *The Shadow of Christ in the Law of Moses* (Phillipsburg, NJ: P&R, 1991), 43.
14. Fairbairn, *Typology of Scripture*, 54.
15. Matthew 11:11.
16. Fairbairn, *Typology of Scripture*, 149.
17. John 14:6.
18. Poythress, *The Shadow of Christ in the Law of Moses*, 11.
19. Matthew 16:3–4.
20. Romans 5:12–17.
21. Hebrews 10:1; 8:5; Colossians 2:16–17.
22. 1 Peter 3:21.
23. Colossians 2:20; Galatians 3:24; 4:3.
24. Matthew 12:41–42.
25. Greidanus, *Preaching Christ from the Old Testament*, 251.
26. Poythress, *The Shadow of Christ in the Law of Moses*, 39.
27. Jonah 2; Matthew 12:39–40.
28. 2 Corinthians 1:21; 1 Corinthians 11:4; 1 Peter 2:9; Revelation 1:6.
29. Fairbairn, *Typology of Scripture*, 44; Matthew 19:28; Revelation 7:4–17; 12:14; 15:8.
30. John 1:14; Hebrews 9:8–9; Revelation 21:3.

CHAPTER 14: CHRIST'S PROMISES: DISCOVERING JESUS IN THE

OLD TESTAMENT COVENANTS

1. Jeremiah 31:31–34.
2. Luke 22:20.
3. Walter C Kaiser, "The Old Promise and the New Covenant," *Journal of the Evangelical Theological Society,* http://www.etsjets.org/files/JETS-PDFs/15/15-1/15-1-pp011-023_JETS.pdf, accessed February 11, 2013.
4. Westminster Confession of Faith, 7.5.
5. Ibid., 7.3, 5.
6. Genesis 3:14–15.
7. Genesis 9:8–17.
8. Genesis 12–17.
9. Exodus 19–20.
10. 2 Samuel 7.
11. Jeremiah 31:31–34; Luke 22:20.
12. O. Palmer Robertson, *The Christ of the Covenants* (Phillipsburg, NJ: 1980), 25.
13. Genesis 6:5.
14. Genesis 16.
15. Exodus 16–17; 32.
16. 2 Samuel 23:1–5 KJV.
17. Leviticus 26; Deuteronomy 28.
18. Luke 22:20.
19. Genesis 3:15.
20. Genesis 9:9.
21. Genesis 15:1 KJV.
22. Genesis 12:1–3.
23. Exodus 19:4–5.
24. Exodus 20:1–2.
25. 2 Samuel 7.
26. Galatians 4:4–5 KJV.
27. Genesis 4.
28. Genesis 8:20–9:10.
29. Jeremiah 34:18–20.
30. Genesis 15:9–21.
31. Exodus 20:24.
32. Exodus 24:8.
33. 2 Samuel 7:14.
34. Luke 22:20.
35. Genesis 8:22; 9:11, 15.
36. Genesis 17:4–8.
37. Exodus 19:6.
38. Matthew 26:28.
39. Matthew 26:26–28.
40. John 8:33–43.

41. Galatians 3:7.
42. Revelation 21:22–23 KJV.
43. Revelation 21:3.
44. Revelation 21:7.
45. Matthew 28:19–20.
46. John 1:14 KJV.
47. Jeremiah 31:32–34.
48. Matthew 26:28.
49. Jeremiah 31:31–32.
50. Jeremiah 31:32–34.
51. Hebrews 8:10.
52. Matthew 1:23.
53. Revelation 21:3–5.

CHAPTER 15: CHRIST'S PROVERBS: DISCOVERING JESUS IN THE OLD TESTAMENT PROVERBS

1. Luke 24:27.
2. Colossians 3:16.
3. Luke 11:31.
4. Proverbs 27:5–6.
5. Proverbs 27:1.
6. Matthew 6:31–34.
7. Raymond Dillard and Tremper Longman, *An Introduction to the Old Testament* (Grand Rapids: Zondervan, 1994), 245.
8. Proverbs 1:10–12.
9. Proverbs 6:30–31; 30:17.
10. Proverbs 20:26; 12:10.
11. Proverbs 2:22; 22:3.
12. Proverbs 4:7–9; 11:18–19.
13. Proverbs 12:7; 15:6.
14. Proverbs 30:4.
15. Throughout Proverbs, *Wisdom* is personified as a female. This makes no statement about the gender of God, but reflects the feminine gender of the Hebrew noun for *wisdom*.
16. Proverbs 9:1–6.
17. Isaiah 25:6; 55:1–2; Matthew 22:1–14.
18. Proverbs 8:1–21.
19. William Arnot, vol. 1, *Studies in Proverbs* (London: T. Nelson and Sons, 1859), 206.
20. Luke 2:40–52; Matthew 11; John 1; 1 Corinthians 1:30; Colossians 1:15–17; 2:3.
21. Gospel banquet (Matt. 26:26–29; Luke 14:15–23); never-ending feast (Matt. 8:11; Rev. 3:20; 19:9, 17–19).
22. John 1:1–4; Hebrews 1:2.

23. Mark 2:19.
24. John 16:25 KJV.
25. Matthew 7:24.
26. E.g., Proverbs 1:16 and Romans 3:15; Proverbs 3:7 and Romans 12:16; Proverbs 3:11 and Hebrews 12:5.

CHAPTER 16: CHRIST'S POETS: DISCOVERING JESUS IN THE OLD TESTAMENT POEMS

1. Luke 24:44.
2. Shield (Ps. 28:7), Rock (Ps. 18:2), Shepherd (Ps. 23:1), Judge (Ps. 7:11), Refuge (Ps. 46:1), Fortress (Ps. 31:3), Creator (Ps. 8:1, 6), Healer (Ps. 30:2), Provider (Ps. 78:23–29), Redeemer (Ps. 107:2).
3. Luke 24:25–27, 44.
4. Derek Kidner, *Psalms 1–72* (London: InterVarsity Press, 1973), 24.
5. Joel R. Beeke and Anthony T. Selvaggio, eds., *Sing a New Song* (Grand Rapids: Reformation Heritage Books, 2010), 135.
6. Ibid., 159.
7. Ibid.
8. 1 Peter 1:10–12.
9. Leyland Ryken and Tremper Longman III, eds., *The Complete Literary Guide to the Bible* (Grand Rapids: Zondervan, 1993), 252, citing John Calvin.
10. Acts 2:25.
11. Acts 2:30–31.
12. Psalm 2.
13. Luke 20:41–44.
14. John Calvin, *Commentary on the Psalms* vol. 4 (Grand Rapids: Baker Book House, 1996), 295–96.
15. E.g., Psalms 22.
16. Christopher J. H. Wright, *Knowing Jesus through the Old Testament* (Downers Grove, IL: IVP, 1992), 241–42.
17. E.g., Psalms 22:1 and Matthew 27:46; Psalms 31:5 and Luke 23:46; Psalms 110:1 and Matthew 22:44.
18. Beeke and Selvaggio, *Sing a New Song*, 159, citing Geerhardus Vos.
19. Psalms 8; 24; 29; 33; 47; 48.
20. Psalms 39; 51; 86; 120.
21. Psalms 22; 69.
22. Psalms 18; 66; 107; 118; 138.
23. Psalms 121; 131.
24. Psalms 78; 105; 106; 136.
25. Psalms 22; 69.
26. Psalms 2; 20; 21; 24; 45; 47.
27. Matthew 23:13–39.
28. Young boy (Ps. 8:2); teenager (Ps. 119:9); the synagogue (Ps. 5:7);

morning devotions (Ps. 5:3); the Scriptures (Ps. 12:6); His preaching (Ps. 40:9); defeated temptation (Ps. 91:7); He woke (Ps. 3:5); He slept (Ps. 4:8); the Devil at work (Ps. 10:8–9); souls saved (Ps. 3:8); deaths of followers (Ps. 12:1); the Passover (Ps. 118:17–29); the cross (Ps. 55:4–5); falsely accused (Ps. 2:1–2); betrayed (Ps. 55:12–14); forsaken (Ps. 22:1); dying, then rising again (Ps. 16:10–11).

29. Michael Lefebvre, *Singing the Songs of Jesus* (Tain, Ross-shire: Christian Focus, 2010), 92–93.

30. Luke 24:27; 44–48.

31. Ephesians 5:22–33; Psalm 45.

32. Adultery (Ex. 34:10–17), theme taken up by prophets (Isa. 51:1–17; 54:6; 61:10; 62:4–5; Jer. 2:1–3; 31:32; Mal. 2:14), carried into the New Testament (Matt. 9:15; Luke 5:35; John 3:29; 2 Cor. 11:2; Rev. 19:7; 21:9; 22:17).

33. Revelation 21–22.

34. Vern Poythress, *The Shadow of Christ in the Law of Moses* (Phillipsburg, NJ: P&R, 1991), 38–39.

35. James Hamilton, "The Messianic Music of the Song of Songs," *Westminster Theological Journal* 68 (2006), 337.

STUDY QUESTIONS

1. John 5:46.
2. John 5:41–47.
3. 1 Peter 1:11.
4. Hebrews 4:2.
5. Luke 24:25.
6. Colossians 1:16.
7. 2 Corinthians 5:17.
8. Hebrews 1:14.
9. Psalm 19:1–6; Romans 1:18–21.
10. Hebrews 12:1–3, 22–24.
11. Exodus 33:20; 1 Timothy 6:15–16; 1 John 4:12.
12. John Calvin, *Institutes* 4.8.5, John T. McNeill, ed. Ford Lewis Battles, trans. (Philadelphia: Westminster Press, 1960), 349.
13. Acts 7:38.

ACKNOWLEDGMENTS

1. Ephesians 3:8–12.

SCRIPTURE INDEX

SUBJECT INDEX

ABOUT THE AUTHOR

David Murray was a pastor in Scotland for twelve years before crossing "the pond" in 2007 to take up his present position as Professor of Old Testament and Practical Theology at Puritan Reformed Theological Seminary. He is the author of *Christians Get Depressed Too* and *How Sermons Work*. He is also president of HeadHeartHand Media, a small Christian film company that has produced two DVDs: *God's Technology* and *CrossReference: The Angel of the Lord*.

David is married to Shona and they have five children. They all love skiing, fishing, and camping around beautiful Lake Michigan.

He blogs at HeadHeartHand.org and you can follow him on Twitter @DavidPMurray.